Self-Care Journal

'Your mental health is
more important than the test,
the interview, the lunch
date, the meeting, the family
dinner, the soccer game,
the recital and the grocery run.
Take care of yourself.'

ANONYMOUS

Self-Care Journal

HOW TO MAKE THE MOST
OF YOUR ONE AMAZING LIFE

HERRON

What's Inside

ONE

Know Yourself

11

What does self-care look like to you? *13*
Who are you? *23*
What do you do? *31*
What would you like to do? *45*
What are your values? *67*
Face your limiting beliefs. *83*
Remember the kid you were. *99*
Get into the flow. *107*

TWO

Tuning into Your Senses

119

That smells nice. *121*
Music to my ears. *131*
You are what you taste. *143*
I spy with my little eye. *169*
Let's get physical. *189*
The sixth sense. *205*

THREE

Self-Care Cards

213

52 little (but big) ways to look after yourself. *215*

FOUR

It's a Wrap

243

Now what? *245*

Introduction

Self-care is as easy as meeting your needs. And as hard as meeting your needs. Can you look yourself in the eye and be honest: who am I and what do I need? By answering these questions, you'll develop deeper self-knowledge and build greater self-confidence. You will learn how to make good decisions for yourself and value every single moment of your one wild and amazing life.

To begin, turn the page...

1

KNOW YOURSELF

In this section of the journal, you'll be invited to explore the true nature of your character, consider what you do and don't enjoy in life, get clarity on your values and goals, and work out how you can make more time and space in your life for the things that support and nurture you.

'Keep taking time
for yourself until
you are you again.'

LALAH DELIA

What does self-care look like to you?

The before picture.

Before you jump into this journal, take a minute to think about your current understanding of self-care.

Use the exercises on the following pages to brainstorm and explore what it means to you. Maybe it's a small thing like drinking more water, getting that facial, ditching the guilt when you leave work on time, or something big like training to run a marathon. Whatever it is, take the time to reflect and write it down.

This is the **before** picture.

Often we think we want certain things but if we haven't fully engaged in why we want them, or considered how they are going to nurture our essential selves, actually getting them can make us feel defeated and out of sync.

So do the work up front. Get to know yourself. Work out what really matters. What is right for YOU. Because these days it's pretty easy to get hung up on what everyone else is doing or suggesting. So hang in there. There's plenty of time for bubble baths and girls' nights out, if that's what you decide you want.

But by the time you have finished this journal your **after** picture may look a lot different than you thought or expected.

Use the space provided to jot down your
current ideas about self-care.

My ideas about self-care continued.

My current self-care practices and priorities.

A little quiz.

Take the quiz on these pages to find out how well you are doing at the moment. Repeat this quiz any time if you need to check in with yourself again while working through the journal. Consider photocopying it and placing it somewhere prominent, like on the fridge door. That way you can keep it uppermost in your mind.

	ABSOLUTELY	SOMETIMES	NOT REALLY
1. I spend time with people who make me happy.	○	○	○
2. I am kind to myself and give myself positive affirmations.	○	○	○
3. I get enough sleep.	○	○	○
4. I eat to nourish my body and my mind.	○	○	○
5. I regularly exercise or do a fun physical activity.	○	○	○
6. I have quiet moments where I let my nervous system relax.	○	○	○
7. I make time to be with my thoughts and self-reflect.	○	○	○
8. I take time to express my thoughts or feelings, or have a creative outlet.	○	○	○
9. I say no to extra responsibilities when my plate is already full.	○	○	○
10. I allow myself to show emotions.	○	○	○
11. I spend time with my pets (if applicable)	○	○	○

	ABSOLUTELY	SOMETIMES	NOT REALLY
12. I make time to do responsible things like creating a budget or studying.	○	○	○
13. I take time to organise my life.	○	○	○
14. I spend time with people I love and care about.	○	○	○
15. I regularly unplug from social media.	○	○	○
16. I feel connected to a community.	○	○	○
17. I make time for myself to complete necessary tasks.	○	○	○
18. I take time to chat and get to know others in my community.	○	○	○
19. I set boundaries in my relationships with my partner, family and friends.	○	○	○
20. When necessary, I can say no without feeling guilty.	○	○	○
21. I strive for balance between work, family, relationships, play and relaxation.	○	○	○

	ABSOLUTELY	SOMETIMES	NOT REALLY
22. I do something each week that gives me a sense of joy.	○	○	○
23. I visualise my dreams and goals regularly.	○	○	○
24. I make space to laugh or play without judgement.	○	○	○
25. I am aware of what my passions are and how I can fit them into my life.	○	○	○

Take note of your answers, particularly where you have ticked 'Not really' or 'Sometimes'. This provides you with areas to focus on as you work through this journal.

*'You don't have to
be perfect
to be amazing.'*

ANONYMOUS

Who are you?

You can't care properly for someone you don't know. In this section you'll get to work through the ins and outs of who exactly you are, so when it comes to looking after yourself, you will know exactly how to do it.

What do you think of you?

Look at the circles opposite and colour in the ones that sound like you.

Don't think too much about it, just go with the first five that shout out.

It's tempting to pick what you think OTHERS would say about you. But that's not relevant here. What do YOU think of YOU?

KIND

FUNNY

HONEST

GENEROUS

PRINCIPLED

ENERGETIC

LOVING

FREE

CAPABLE

WARM

EMPATHETIC

STRONG

THOUGHTFUL

INTELLIGENT

INDEPENDENT

ADVENTUROUS

SOCIABLE

COMPASSIONATE

CURIOUS

use this one to write you own word should you need to

Using the five words you selected from the previous page, write down what each of these characteristics means to you. See the example provided below. Try to go with your gut, but if you need extra inspiration you could try looking at the dictionary definition.

WARM - kind, loving, easy to be around. Greets people with a smile and a hug, knows how to make others feel cared for. Easy going, not quick to anger, has a peaceful energy. Relaxed. Calm.

1.

2.

3.

4.

5.

IF ONLY I WAS ...

It's important to accept and love the person you are, but that doesn't mean you can't grow as a person. Go back to the words on page 25 and note below any character traits that you aspire to. Don't worry if they seem unachievable. Just write them down. Then, on the page opposite, brainstorm what you can do to move in this direction.

FROM LITTLE THINGS BIG THINGS GROW
(ACTIONS I CHOOSE TO HELP MYSELF BE MORE WHO I WANT TO BE)

1. ______________________________

2. ______________________________

3. ______________________________

4. ______________________________

5. ______________________________

6. ______________________________

7. ______________________________

8. ______________________________

‘What you do today determines who you will be tomorrow.’

JOHN SPENCE

What do you do?

This section provides the opportunity to explore the activities that you do day-to-day, week-to-week and even further out than that. When you consider these activities in relation to your character attributes (as explored in the previous section) you can explore with a fresh perspective whether or not they 'suit' your life.

NURTURE YOUR ATTRIBUTES.

It's time to explore the things you do that nurture the positive aspects of yourself. Think of it as ways that your cup gets replenished.

In the left-hand column below write down your 'five attributes' words (from pages 26-27) and in the right-hand column think of one or two activities that support this attribute (My 10 Activities). Try to write down what springs to mind, but if you are stuck for ideas check out the page opposite. (If you prefer, you can colour in the words opposite that appeal to you.)

My 5 Attributes	My 10 Activities
1. ______	______ ______
2. ______	______ ______
3. ______	______ ______
4. ______	______ ______
5. ______	______ ______

GO FOR A HIKE
SING OUT LOUD
READ A BOOK
DRAW (YOU DON'T HAVE TO BE 'GOOD')
GO TO THE OP SHOP
RIDE A BIKE
DO A PUZZLE
GO TO THE MOVIES BY YOURSELF
PICK SOME FLOWERS
STRETCH
SLEEP IN
GARDEN
GO TO CHURCH
GO AWAY FOR THE NIGHT
GO OUT TO DINNER
JUMP IN PUDDLES
WRITE A KIDS' STORY
BAKE
WALK ON THE BEACH
DECLUTTER
ORGANISE YOUR NEXT HOLIDAY
GO SWIMMING
LIGHT A CANDLE
CALL SOMEONE YOU CARE ABOUT AND SAY 'I LOVE YOU'
MEDITATE
JOURNAL
HAVE A PICNIC
PLAY AN INSTRUMENT
DANCE
DELETE ITEMS FROM YOUR TO-DO LIST
MEDITATE
WALK BAREFOOT
GET OUT IN NATURE
WATCH COMEDY ON YOUTUBE
DO A RANDOM ACT OF KINDNESS
WALK IN THE RAIN
DO YOGA
MAKE LOVE
VISIT AN ANIMAL SHELTER
GO CAMPING
HAVE A LITTLE LIE DOWN
DONATE BLOOD
BUILD SOMETHING
START A NEW SPORT
MAKE A VISION BOARD
CALL YOUR MUM OR DAD
LEARN TO SURF
CLEAN THE HOUSE
GO FOR A RUN
PAT THE CAT
CATCH UP WITH FRIENDS
MAKE A PLAN
GO TO BED EARLY
GET A TATTOO
LOOK AT THE CLOUDS AND DAYDREAM
DO SOME CRAFT
TAKE PHOTOS

How often do you do what makes you tick?

In the previous page, you identified 10 activities that are in tune with who you are. But how often do you engage in them?

Let's make some lists to find out, considering how frequently you did these 10 activities in the past year, month, week and day.

Using the page opposite, list the activities, starting with the ones you did most frequently. If you like, you can write frequency in brackets after the activity, such as 'went surfing (daily)' or 'caught up with friends (weekly)'.

LAST YEAR, I...

1.

2.

3.

4.

5.

6.

7.

8.

9.

10.

LAST MONTH, I...

1.

2.

3.

4.

5.

6.

7.

8.

9.

10.

LAST WEEK, I...

1.

2.

3.

4.

5.

6.

7.

8.

9.

10.

TODAY, I...

1.

2.

3.

4.

5.

6.

7.

8.

9.

10.

REVIEW YOUR LISTS

Take a moment to review your lists. How do they make you feel? Do you want to diversify or are you happy with what you do and how often you do it?

Write down your reflections below.

WHAT WAS MISSING FROM YOUR LISTS?

Write down six things that aren't on any of your lists – but you wish were. Try not to make them big-ticket items (like an all-expenses-paid holiday in Tahiti) but things that are possible within the structure of your life ... or the life you are working towards.

1. ______________________________

2. ______________________________

3. ______________________________

4. ______________________________

5 ______________________________

6 ______________________________

NOTES AND REFLECTIONS

Learn something new.

Learning is good for your brain. New neural pathways form and electrical impulses shoot faster along them as you process new information. Learning helps build confidence and can provide an environment in which to meet others, helping satisfy our human need for connection. Plus, learning stimulates creativity as new information and new perspectives help us join the dots in new ways. Whether it's a sport, musical instrument, craft activity or something heady like writing or blogging, learning a new skill is good for you.

On the page opposite write down a list of things you'd like to learn. Brainstorm everything you can imagine. Don't hold back!

Circle the top three.

Investigate how to make it happen.

Make a plan and do it.

'I simply remember a
few of my favourite
things and then
I don't feel so bad...'

FROM *THE SOUND OF MUSIC*

What would you like to do?

What are a few of your favourite things? Are they present enough in your day-to-day life? And how do they make you feel? Conversely, what is truly a bore for you and that you'd love to offload?

The exercises in this section will help you to reconnect with the idea of your favourite things and to have ownership over what you prioritise and deprioritise in your life.

FUN FAVOURITE THINGS BRAINSTORM

Kids love to ask and talk about their favourites – colours, flowers, toys, teddies. But somewhere along the road to adulthood we forget to keep in mind our favourite things and to pursue them with childlike enthusiasm.

What's your favourite colour?

Which is your favourite season?

What's your favourite city?

What's your favourite possession?

What's your favourite fruit?

Who is your favourite person to have a coffee with?

What's your favourite dessert?

What's your favourite bird?

What's your favourite comfort meal?

What's your favourite quote?

What's your favourite month of the year?

What's your favourite song when you are feeling down?

Who is your favourite relative?

What's your favourite outdoor activity?

What's your favourite smell?

What's your favourite indoor activity?

What's your favourite emotion?

Who's your favourite movie star?

Who's your favourite comedian?

Who is your favourite celebrity chef?

What was your favourite job?

What's your favourite flower?

What's your favourite beach?

What's your favourite piece of trivia?

What's your favourite colour of smoothie?

What's your favourite take-away meal?

What's your all-time favourite band?

What's your favourite holiday?

What's your favourite cake flavour?

What's your favourite place to eat out?

What's your favourite piece of summer clothing?

What's your current favourite TV show?

Favourite places and things.

What are some of your favourite places or things, and how do they make you feel? Think of places you go or things you do regularly (or would like to). They don't have to be extravagant – one of them could be your home or your backyard.

1. Write each favourite place or thing in the top half of the circles opposite.

2. Think about how each place or thing makes you feel. Write this word in the bottom section of the circle. Narrow it down to just one word to help you home in on what makes it good.

3. Listen to your own thoughts in regard to the emotions you feel but if you are stuck, here are some ideas to get you thinking …

CALM, ENERGISED, HOPEFUL, STRONG
CONNECTED (TO SELF OR NATURE), MOTIVATED,
RESPECTED, PROUD, EXCITED, FREE.

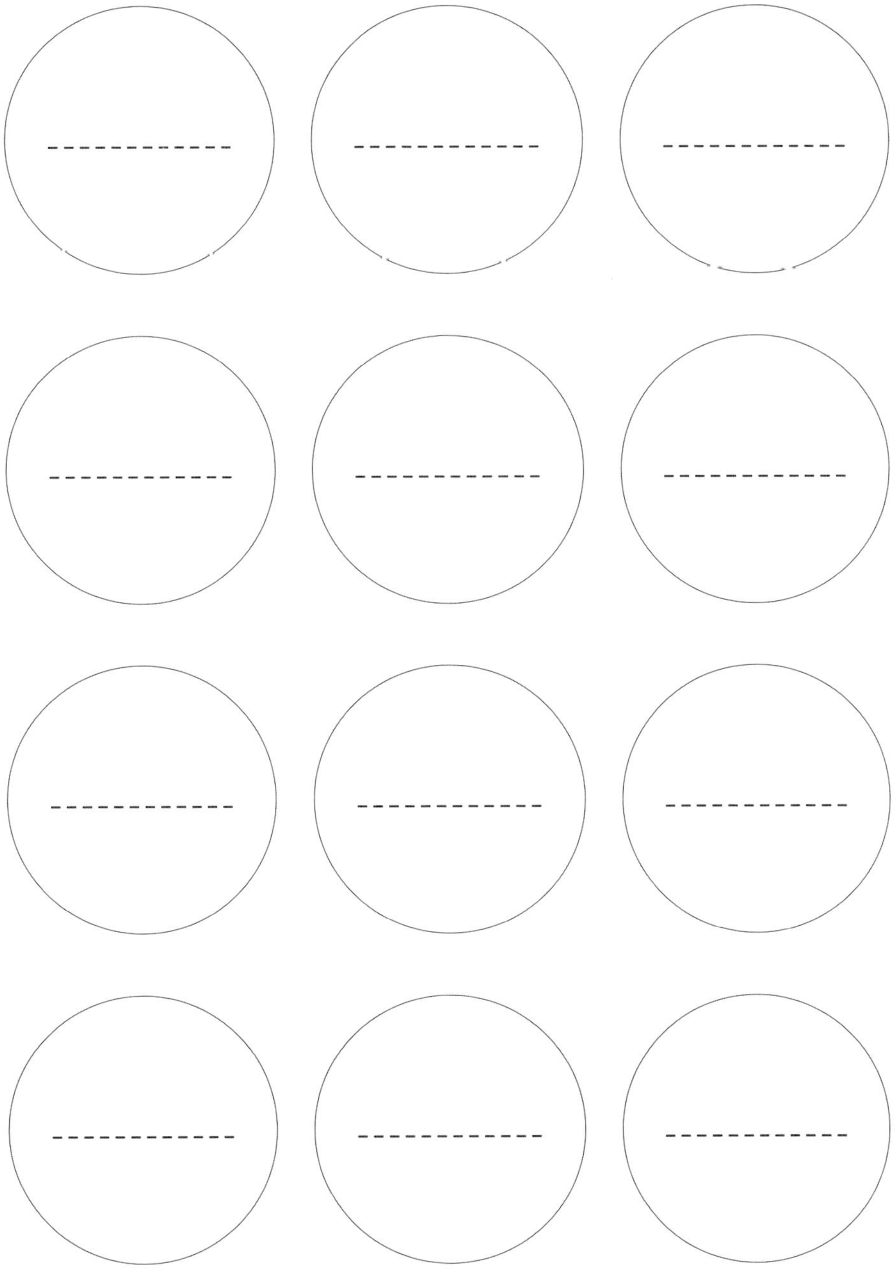

My emotions.

Emotions are often linked to colours – most obviously red for love (and anger), blue for calm, yellow for happiness – and they are essentially connected to the chakras in the body, where many people believe we store our emotions. It can be helpful to think of our emotions in terms of colour, for ease of reference and recall.

Look at the emotions you put in the circles on the previous page.

The circle opposite is divided into 12 sections. Select a colour for each chosen emotion from the previous page, and then colour in a segment of this circle for each emotion. (If you have repeated emotions on page 49, simply repeat the colour in another segment).

COLOUR WHEEL OF EMOTIONS

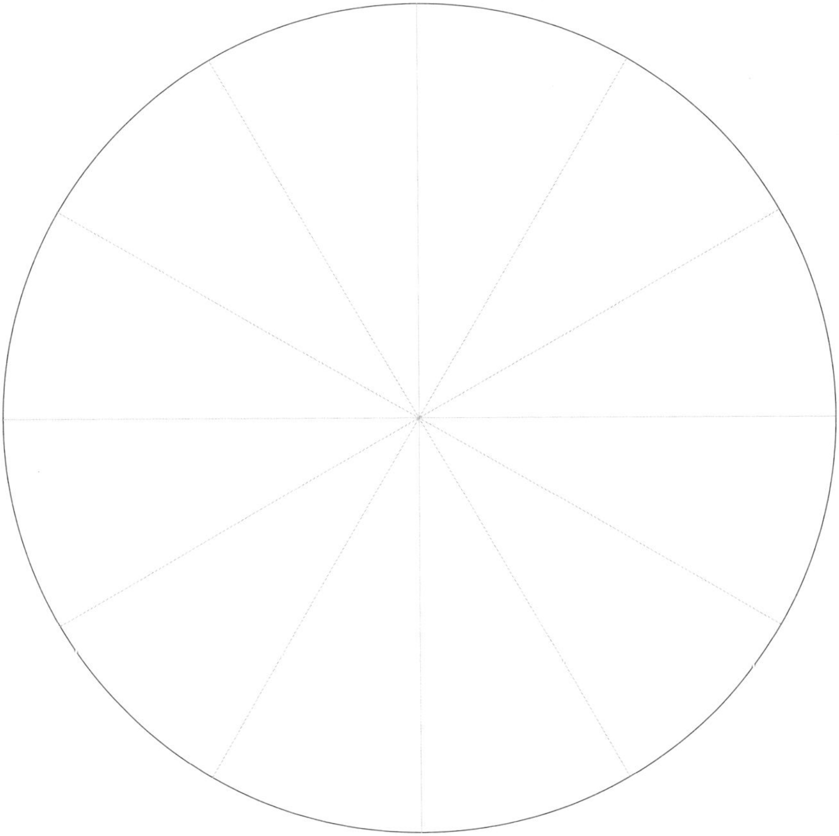

NOTES AND REFLECTIONS

Consider your colour wheel on page 51. Is there a common theme? Are the same one or two emotions coming up again and again or is it a mixed bag? Do these emotions resonate with you? Are you happy that these feelings predominate in your life? Is anything missing? Use these pages to note your answers and any other reflections on this exercise.

WISH LIST ACTIVITIES

In the bold circles at the top of the page opposite, write the 4 'feeling states' (such as 'calm' or 'energised') that matter the most to you. These words should sum up how you want to feel most of the time.

Then in the circles below brainstorm your wish list activities – all the things that you would love to do but for whatever reason don't.

Draw a line from the activity to the emotion that best suits it.

NOTES AND REFLECTIONS

Consider your wish list activities from the previous page. Which activities ones best align with your desired feeling states, and therefore, which ones are most relevant for you? Use this space to reflect on this question, and to brainstorm ideas for how you can introduce or do more of these activities in your day-to-day life.

DITCH LIST ACTIVITIES

Let's try that exercise again. But this time consider less desirable feeling states, particularly in relation to things you do day-in-day-out that may provoke these emotions. Maybe the feelings are frustration, boredom, anger. Be honest. Write these 4 feeling states in the bold circles at the top of page 59.

Then in the circles below write your day-to-day activities – all the things that you have to do, but would probably rather not. It could be organising that never-ending stack of papers, cleaning the bathroom, emptying the bins, cooking dinner, clearing the dishes before bed, monitoring your screen time, grabbing five minutes to exercise.

Draw a line from the activity to the emotion that best suits it.

NOTES AND REFLECTIONS

Consider your ditch list activities from the previous page. Which activities really light up the map, providing a short-circuit to your negative feeling states?

Use this space to reflect on this question, and to brainstorm ideas for how you can introduce some positive changes. Do you have to do all of these things? What can you do to make them easier? Are there ways to automate some of them, plan more effectively or pay someone to help you? If you do have to do them, can you take a more mindful approach?

'Don't ask what the
world needs.
Ask what makes you come
alive and go do it.
Because what the
world needs is more people
who have come alive.'

HOWARD THURMAN

My Self-Care Commitments

I WILL DO MORE ...

I WILL DO LESS ...

'You cannot change what you are, only what you do.'

PHILIP PULLMAN

'Values are like
fingerprints.
Nobody's are the same,
but you leave 'em all
over everything
you do.'

ELVIS PRESLEY

What are your values?

Ah **values**, the word sounds so important, weighty, like rules your Grandma laid down or something from the tax department that you can't quite understand.

They can also be a bit slippery. You might think you've got them sorted but as you get older, or significant things happen in your life, then they can change. Or they might stay the same.

So it's important to keep analysing your values. And consequently you don't need to be scared of them. They are not tattoos; you can outgrow what once seemed unwavering.

How do you know what your values are?

Value can be a bit nebulous. They linger in your subconscious, driving your thoughts, decisions and actions, often without you even realising. This is where the self-care part comes in. If you don't know your values, how are you going to be in charge of your life, and allow yourself the care that you need? You risk being led by invisible forces and then wonder why your needs aren't being met.

Unless of course you take control.

Take some time to reflect on values. A value is not an outcome, such as a good job or lots of money, but a standard to live by – something you think is important, such as family, honesty, accountability, fairness, independence, loyalty – the options are many.

Look to the past for clues: times you've achieved, or felt proud, or not. Was there something then that chimed or clashed with your values? Find that which chimed. Write it down. Hold it close.

Think of someone you know who inspires you.
What characteristics do they have?

Think of a public figure who inspires you.
What characteristics do they have?

What are you proud of? Why?

When you feel unfulfilled win your life, what is missing?

Who or what makes your blood boil? Why?

If you could choose one thing to change about the world right now, what would it be, and what does this tell you about yourself?

CHOOSE YOUR VALUES

Considering your answers to the previous questions, look at the list below. Which values resonate? Circle with a pen, or place a tick alongside.

ACCURACY	COMPASSION	EMPATHY	GENEROSITY
ACHIEVEMENT	CONFIDENCE	ENDURANCE	GOODNESS
ADAPTABILITY	CONSISTENCY	ENERGY	GRACE
ADVENTURE	COURAGE	ENVIRONMENT	GRATITUDE
ART	COURTESY	EQUALITY	GROWTH
ALTRUISM	CREATIVITY	ETHICALITY	HAPPINESS
AMBITION	CREDIBILITY	FAIRNESS	HARD WORK
ASSERTIVENESS	CURIOSITY	FAMILY	HARMONY
BALANCE	DECISIVENESS	FAME	HEALTH
BEAUTY	DEDICATION	FIDELITY	HONESTY
BRAVERY	DEPENDABILITY	FINANCIAL FREEDOM	HOPE
CALM	DETERMINATION	FOCUS	HUMILITY
CERTAINTY	DEVOTION	FORESIGHT	HUMOUR
CLEANLINESS	DIGNITY	FREEDOM	IMAGINATION
COMMITMENT	DISCIPLINE	FRIENDSHIP	INDEPENDENCE
COMMON SENSE	EFFICIENCY	FUN	INDIVIDUALITY

INNOVATION

INQUISITIVENESS

INSPIRATION

INTEGRITY

INTIMACY

JUSTICE

KINDNESS

KNOWLEDGE

LEADERSHIP

LOGIC

LOVE

LOYALTY

MEANING

MODERATION

MOTIVATION

OPENNESS

OPTIMISM

ORDER

ORIGINALITY

PARENTING

PASSION

PATIENCE

PEACE

PERSISTENCE

PLAYFULNESS

POISE

POWER

PRODUCTIVITY

PROFESSIONALISM

PURPOSE

QUALITY

REALISM

REASON

RECOGNITION

RECREATION

REFLECTION

RELATIONSHIPS

RESPECT

RESPONSIBILITY

RESTRAINT

REVERENCE

RISK

SATISFACTION

SECURITY

SELF-RELIANCE

SENSITIVITY

SERENITY

SERVICE

SHARING

SIGNIFICANCE

SILENCE

SIMPLICITY

SINCERITY

SKILFULNESS

SOLITUDE

SPIRITUALITY

SPONTANEITY

STABILITY

STRENGTH

STRUCTURE

SUCCESS

SUPPORT

SUSTAINABILITY

TEAMWORK

TEMPERANCE

THANKFULNESS

THOROUGHNESS

THOUGHTFULNESS

TOLERANCE

TOUGHNESS

TRADITION

TRANQUILLITY

TRANSPARENCY

TRUST

TRUTH

UNDERSTANDING

UNIQUENESS

UNITY

VISION

VITALITY

WEALTH

WELCOMENESS

WISDOM

WONDER

Set goals based on your values.

When you set goals based on your values, you're much more likely to achieve them. Why? Because you want to. And your whole self is backing you. There's no confusion or disconnection.

Now that you are more in tune with your values, consider some of your self-care goals. (See the following pages for tips on goal-setting.) What would you like to do more regularly or consistently? Is there something specific you'd like to achieve? Or something you'd like to stop doing?

Use the page on the right to specify up to four self-care goals, then assign a value (or more than one if you like) to each goal. Does the value ring true to you? Is it something you prioritise? If not why not? Perhaps you need to reconsider that goal?

If a goal has a clear value assigned to it, that's great! Does having that value attached to the goal makes it feel more achievable? Do you understand better how it fits into your life and why it is important?

GOAL	VALUE
1.	
2.	
3.	
4.	

Goal setting 101.

Goals need to be specific and tangible, and setting them is easy when you know how. Here's some steps to follow to help make a clear path to success.

STEP 1: create a vision board

The first part of goal setting is to create a vision board. This is a fun activity where you get to pull together all the things that inspire you – ideas, words, people, objects – into one place. This will frame your goal in a visual way. Put it on the wall or somewhere special and use it to stay motivated.

STEP 2: make the plan

Here's the nitty gritty – where you specify exactly what it is that you want to achieve and how you are going to do it.

Give your goal a nickname – it's friendlier and more memorable that way. Think of your goal like your buddy on this journey.

Describe in words exactly what your goal is. Make this description S.M.A.R.T. That's probably an acronym you've heard before. It stands for: ***Specific*** *(clear, unambiguous and well defined).* ***Measurable*** *(there are ways you can* *track your progress).* ***Achievable*** *(it can be done)* ***Relevant*** *(the purpose behind the goal is clear and the goal will deliver it).* ***Timely*** *(with a clear beginning and end point).*

Set your milestones – break your ultimate goal down into smaller goals and set targets on achieving these. This will help you stay focussed and give you positive reinforcement along the way.

Identify what you need to do – to achieve each milestone you will need to complete certain tasks. Document those tasks in as much detail as you can.

STEP 3: know when you've nailed it

Write down how you imagine success and how it is going to make you feel – the more you understand what success is, the more likely you are to get there. Preparing an outcome statement is a powerful tool that you can use to stay motivated. Pick a reward to celebrate with at the end of the process – you will deserve it.

Don’t forget proud moments.

Before you embark on new goals it’s good to remember past ones that you have successfully achieved. Remembering these can give us the courage to believe in ourselves. It’s easy to forget proud moments. The next hurdle comes hot on its heels, and we become burdened by the current set of challenges, forgetting how far we’ve come.

Even if you are a young person, you’ve already achieved so much.

Think of five key moments in your life, when you felt proud of yourself. Even if you can’t remember actually feeling that way at the time, in hindsight you know it was a big deal. It might have been when you were six and first rode your bike without training wheels, finishing high school or getting your first job.

Use the page opposite to draw a little doodle of each moment, or write about it in words if you prefer.

See if you can track down photos of these moments. Print them out, put them on the fridge or in frames on a wall that you see regularly.

Remember how far you’ve already come.

1.
PROUD MOMENT

I am proud of...

2.
PROUD MOMENT

I am proud of...

3.
PROUD MOMENT

I am proud of...

4.
PROUD MOMENT

I am proud of...

5.
PROUD MOMENT

Proudest moment ever (go on just choose one) ...

'You can go to the gym,
drink your water,
and take your vitamins,
but if you don't deal with
the sh*t going on in
your heart and head,
you're still going to
be unhealthy.'

ANONYMOUS

Face your limiting beliefs.

A limiting belief is something you think that constrains you. Whether or not you're conscious of it, it's stopping you from achieving what you want.

If there's an outcome that you don't like, think of it this way: something you thought about yourself contributed to that outcome. So what was it? Play detective, dig deep.

Learn to recognise your limiting beliefs and reframe them into something positive that you can achieve. Change is within you. It's possible.

What are your limiting beliefs?

Look at the circles opposite. Which are your demons? Try to identify the worst offenders. We are all a little bit of everything sometimes, so go for the ones that really hold you back. Or are particularly problematic at this moment in your life.

Try to focus on the words that that grab YOU, not what others might think or say. If your family or housemates are constantly telling you that you're messy, but it doesn't bother you, leave it off. Without the heart behind it you will never have the stamina to tackle it head on.

IMPATIENT

DISORGANISED

QUICK TO GIVE UP

LACKING IN CONCENTRATION

COMPULSIVE

IMPULSIVE

DEFENSIVE

FUSSY

I am ...

MESSY

SOCIALLY AWKWARD

ADDICTED TO SOCIAL MEDIA

STUBBORN

RECKLESS

INDECISIVE

A WORKAHOLIC

UNMOTIVATED

FEARFUL

WORRIED

SCARED OF COMMITMENT

PESSIMISTIC

Choose five limiting beliefs from the previous page (or something else not listed there) and write them into the circles in the left hand column. In the right hand column write the opposite attribute.

For example if you've listed IMPATIENT as one of your limiting beliefs, write PATIENT in the circle next to it.

Then on the facing page write a statement or series of statements that present this opposing view.

If your words are IMPATIENT, DISORGANISED, FUSSY, UNMOTIVATED, ADDICTED TO SOCIAL MEDIA, your statement will be: **I am a patient, organised, easy-going, motivated person, who is in control of my social media use.**

Make this your morning mantra.

Write it big and consider decorating the page. Give it your personal stamp. Perhaps bookmark or photocopy the page so it is easy for you to look at when you wake up in the morning.

I am ...

Target your negative self-talk.

Start by listening to the voice inside your head. What is she saying?

Everyone has a different set of statements that are often set on repeat. These can cause downward spirals of self-doubt and negativity and get in the way of you taking care of yourself.

Set a timer for five minutes and get writing. Write down all the negative statements about yourself that jump into your thoughts on a regular basis.

Don't edit them as you go. Just write.

Ready? Set.

Go.

WRITE YOURSELF A NICE LETTER

Reflect on what you've just written. And challenge these thoughts. Are these statements objectively true?

Imagine you are a good friend and have just read your words. Use the space below to write yourself a letter as if you were that friend. What would you say in response?

Create affirmations.

An affirmation is a statement of truth as you want to see it. It embodies confidence and plays an important role in breaking patterns of negative thoughts, words and actions. It's believed that repeating affirmations elevates feel-good hormones and creates new patterns in the brain, promoting positive thought.

The best thing about affirmations is that they can be absolutely anything you want. See the page opposite for some ideas to get your started or, better still, see the next page for some simple rules you can follow to make your own.

Keep your affirmation in mind, repeat it during a ritual (such as meditation) or write it on a note and keep it in your purse.

I am overflowing with joy

My body is healthy; my mind is sharp; my soul is peaceful

I wash away anger and replace it with love

I forgive anyone who has wronged me and peacefully detach

My spirit leads me towards positive choices

My relationship is becoming stronger every day

Creative energy drives me to produce great ideas

My potential for success is limitless

I am loved and lovable

I am admired and I inspire others

I know my worth and my confidence is soaring

Difficult times will pass and I will emerge stronger

I am at peace with all that is happening, has happened and will happen

I am in control of my reactions

It is in my nature to be happy

My life is a gift and I am grateful for everything I have

I attract abundance in all aspects of my life

My body is perfect just the way it is

I have the capacity to meet any challenge calmly and successfully

To create an affirmation, bear in mind these tips:

1. Start with the words 'I am.' These two little words pack a big powerful punch.

2. Use the present tense. (As if you already have achieved what you desire.)

3. Affirm what you want, not what you don't want. And be specific. For example, say: 'I am living in a tidy house', rather than 'I am not a messy person'. Your subconscious doesn't hear the word 'not', only 'messy person', and continues being messy.

4. Be brief, so that your affirmation is memorable.

5. Include at least one 'feeling word'.

6. Always make the affirmation for yourself, not for the benefit of anybody else.

In the boxes opposite write four positive affirmations. Photocopy the page and keep each one in easy reach, so you can access them whenever you need.

Example affirmation: I am grateful that I am earning my target income.

REMEMBER:

REMEMBER:

REMEMBER:

REMEMBER:

Say no.

Chances are saying no is hard for you. That's true for most of us, as we try to meet the needs of others or appear accomplished. But learning to say no with confidence and certainty, on a regular basis, is a kind of superpower.

When saying no, say no. Learn not to offer up excuses as an add-on.

When people ask why, try honesty, not excuses. If you are feeling overloaded and on the edge, say that. Chances are it will elicit greater sympathy than an excuse would.

Do the work first of deciding if and why you are saying no.

It's much easier for the no-giver and the no-receiver if the no is a short and simple.

If appropriate you could offer an alternative. For example, 'I can't make it on Monday. How about Tuesday at 10am instead?' If it's a flat-out no, you are completely within your rights to simply say 'No, thank you'.

Are you worried you will offend somebody? Well if the person is offended, guess what? You are not responsible for that and it may give you a clue that this isn't the best relationship for you.

Practise saying no – try it out on those closest to you first. You could even word them up that it's what you are doing and get feedback from loved ones on your approach.

Saying no is a habit that you need to cultivate. Keep practising and the superpower will be yours.

PRACTISE SAYING NO

(photocopy this page first so you can use more than once and keep track of your progress)

What was the situation?

How did you say no?

How did you feel?

On a scale of 1-10 (with 10 being awesome), how well was this situation resolved?

What would you do differently next time?

'When we are children we seldom think of the future.'

PATRICK ROTHFUSS

Remember the kid you were.

Thinking about who you were as a child, and the events and character of your childhood, can help you understand the person you are today.

It may also take you back to your essence, to a time before the responsibilities of adulthood or the rules of society came to dominate your life.

Conversely, sometimes it's not till we are adults and can escape from the expectations of our parents that we can truly become who we want to be.

So let's take a trip down memory lane and see what there is to learn...

WRITE A MEMORY FROM YOUR CHILDHOOD IN WHICH YOU WERE DOING SOMETHING YOU LOVED.

Would that same activity/moment bring you joy if you were to do it today?

YES ☐ **NO** ☐

What was the essence of the activity – and does this still matter to you?

WHAT DID YOU WISH FOR AS A CHILD?

1. ______________________________ ☐

2. ______________________________ ☐

3. ______________________________ ☐

4. ______________________________ ☐

5. ______________________________ ☐

6. ______________________________ ☐

7. ______________________________ ☐

8. ______________________________ ☐

Tick the boxes if these wishes are still relevant today, and you'd like to find a way to pursue them.

WHAT OTHER ACTIVITIES FROM CHILDHOOD CAN YOU ADD TO YOUR SELF-CARE SCHEDULE?

(It could be as simple as eating an apple a day.)

1. ______________________________

2. ______________________________

3. ______________________________

4. ______________________________

5. ______________________________

6. ______________________________

7. ______________________________

8. ______________________________

9. ______________________________

10. ______________________________

'Passion is energy. Feel the power that comes from focusing on what excites you.'

OPRAH WINFREY

MINDFULNESS MOMENT

Slow down.

Kids live to their own rhythm – sometimes running around like headless chooks, other times taking forever to do nothing much. Take walking down the street. It can sometimes be a very slow affair.

What are they doing exactly?

Looking for treasure

Foraging for beautiful leaves

Stopping to watch a cat

Practising that skateboarding move

Daydreaming

Smelling the flowers

Next time you find yourself rushing somewhere, try to be like a kid. Take in what's around you, notice small things and appreciate the details.

WHAT DID YOU NOTICE WHEN YOU WALKED DOWN THE STREET TODAY?

1.

2.

3.

4.

5.

6.

7.

8.

9.

10.

'Where focus goes,
energy flows.'

TONY ROBBINS

Get into the flow.

Take time out to do something that you can become completely absorbed in – perhaps a puzzle, colouring-in book, exercise, DIY project or even a 'chore' such as sharpening the kitchen knives.

An activity like this provides a good way to take a break and by doing it you may even enter what psychologists call 'flow' (more commonly known as 'being in the zone'), which is when we become so immersed in what we're doing that we temporarily lose touch with time and even our own existence. In a good way.

Your mind is completely connected with your actions, your ideas are flowing, you're achieving, creating, concentrating. The rewards of staying in the moment, finishing what you started, enjoying the creative process and honouring your time are well worth the effort.

Finding the flow.

Kids are pros at time wasting, as any parent knows. But, to steal a favoured kid question: Why? Is it because they are so absorbed in what they are doing – a drawing, a silly game or building a spaceship – that they simply do not want to stop? Perhaps they are in the flow. It's easy for a kid to maintain it, whereas grown-ups are often too busy thinking about what is next.

What do you find so absorbing that you reach the flow state? Perhaps the answer is clear, perhaps you have no idea. Consider the list of common flow-state activities opposite and experiment to find what works for you. Bear in mind that your flow-state activity will be different from others people's depending on your personality type (Google 'personality types and flow state' to find out more about this).

MY FLOW ACTIVITIES

Tick the ones that most appeal to you and next time you have the chance to do this activity, observe the experience and consider if you reached the flow state.

DOING A PUZZLE	DOING SOME CROCHET OR BEADING	DOING A JIGSAW	PLAYING AN INSTRUMENT
SWIMMING	YOGA	MAKING AN ARTWORK	ROCK CLIMBING
COOKING AND BAKING	PAINTING	RUNNING	CYCLING
SURFING	GARDENING	HIKING	DEEP REFLECTION

'Flow is being completely involved in an activity for its own sake. The ego falls away. Time flies. Every action, movement, and thought follows inevitably from the previous one, like playing jazz.'

MIHALY CSIKSZENTMIHALYI

FLOW

Think of the last time you were in the zone.
What was happening? Was it hard to achieve? How did you feel? How did you feel when it was over?

KEEP FLOWING

But remember, flow can't be scheduled. You might set aside an hour to do something you are passionate about and it might not be till the 54th minute that it falls into place. If that's the case remember to ask yourself. Do I have to stop? Or will allowing myself to continue make for a better outcome?

Use this page to document times when you have been in the flow state (that you remember) and reflect on how you were able to maximise and extend the experience.

Distractions be gone.

It's very easy in today's world to get OUT of the flow.

We all know how easy it is to spend 15 minutes scrolling on social media for example. Identify your triggers for distraction and create an 'instead list' of more enjoyable or productive things you could be doing instead. Fill it with fun and engaging ideas, some quick and others that will keep you occupied for a bit longer if needed.

When temptation strikes, go to your instead list and do one of them.

MY INSTEAD LIST

When I am feeling distracted, I can do one of the following activities instead.

1. ____________________

2. ____________________

3. ____________________

4. ____________________

5. ____________________

MINDFULNESS MOMENT

Do some free writing (or doodling).

Using the space provided on the page opposite, choose one of the below activities.

1. Write a poem about a favourite place.

2. Write a short story about an imaginary person.

3. Draw a picture of what is outside your window.

Don't edit it. Don't overthink, just do it and feel what it feels like to freely express yourself without concern for the outcome.

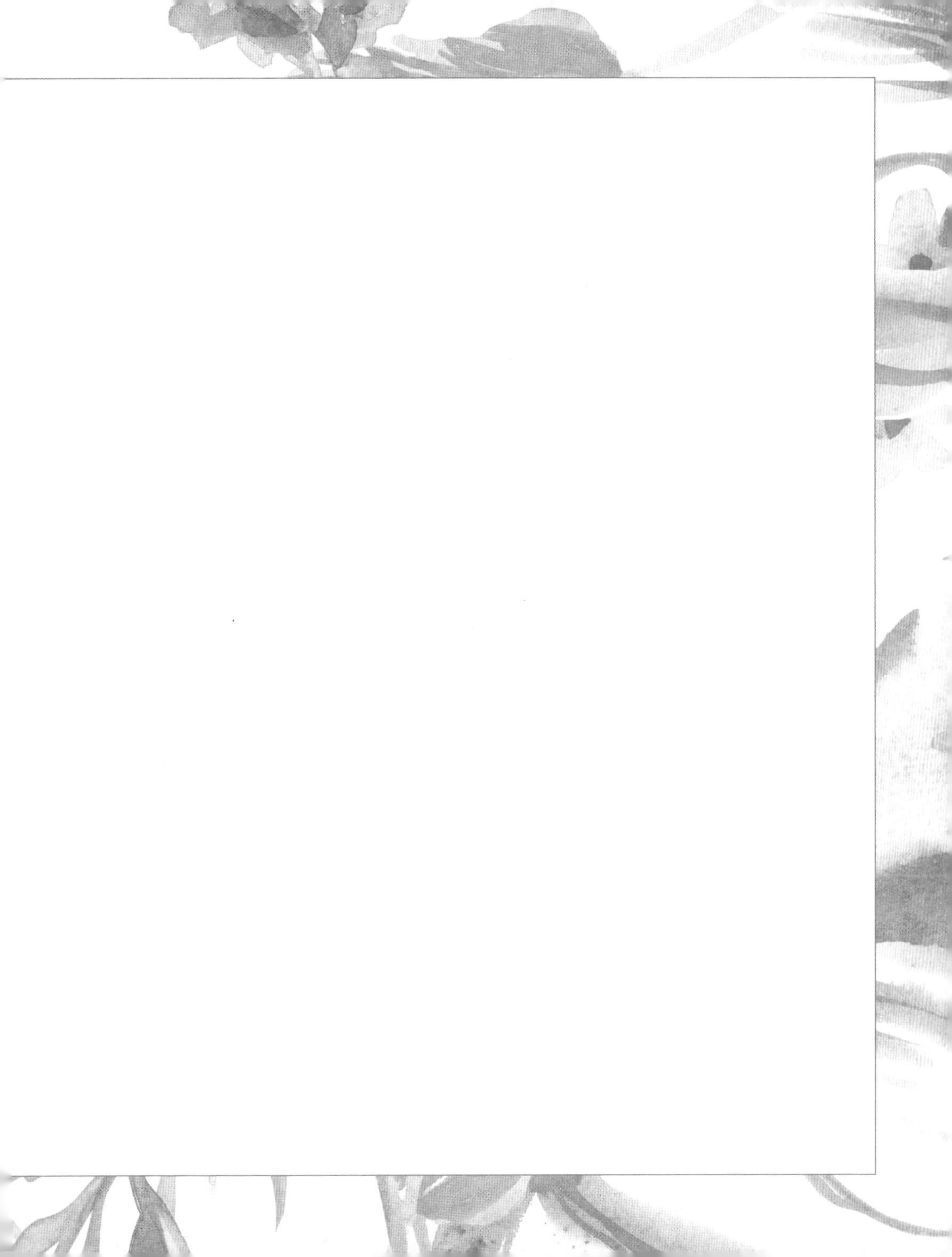

2

TUNING INTO YOUR SENSES

This section of the journal helps you to explore and celebrate your sensory side as you learn to identify the sensations, smells, sounds, tastes, visual treats and physical routines that will soothe, nurture and support you.

'Smell is a potent wizard that transports you across thousands of miles and all the years you have lived.'

HELEN KELLER

That smells nice.

There's something about smell, more so than the other senses perhaps, that catapults you readily to another time and place – a favourite spot, treasured person or a childhood memory. It has transformative magic to it.

What smells resonate with you and how can you harness them to support you in feeling good?

Do a smell audit.

Tune up your nostrils, grab a pen and this journal, and head off on a little sensory walk around your home and garden (if you have one). As you travel around room by room, take notes using the lined space on the following pages. Write down your observations of good, bad and dominant smells, and how you feel in each space based on the smell.

Start as you would your day, in the bedroom. Do you have candles or room fragrance of some kind? Or nothing? Are you happy with this? Move along to the bathroom. Do you choose products based on their smell? Do you have aromatic overload going on? How about your living area? Aromas in the kitchen will change according to what you are cooking, but consider are there meals you make or ingredients you buy simply because of how they smell? Do you have fresh herbs or flowers?

Now go back to the beginning and repeat the process. This time think about how you want each room to smell and the mood you'd like to create. Use whatever words come to mind, even if they might not usually be used to describe smells. For the bedroom you might say, FRESH, CALM, SOFT for example. Write these words in the circles.

BEDROOM

BATHROOM

LAUNDRY

KITCHEN

LIVING AREA

OUTSIDE

Select your smells.

When it comes to creating the right scent to keep you feeling nurtured and nourished you can take inspiration from pretty much anything.

Consider the scents opposite. Think about the 'mood words' you wrote on the previous exercise and consider how each scent feels to you in that regard.

Choose a coloured pencil for each room of your house and colour in the scents listed opposite that appeal to you for that space.

Now consider how to create that smell in each room. Is it the kind of laundry detergent you choose, a scented candle, some fresh flowers, herbs or something else?

SEASONAL SCENTS

Consider if you want different scents at different times of year to help you feel in tune with nature or to switch gears – will the smell of frangipani on a cold winter's day remind you of warm sunny days at the beach?

On the following pages write your recipe of seasonal smells. Don't be limited by the ones listed here, think carefully about what brings you joy.

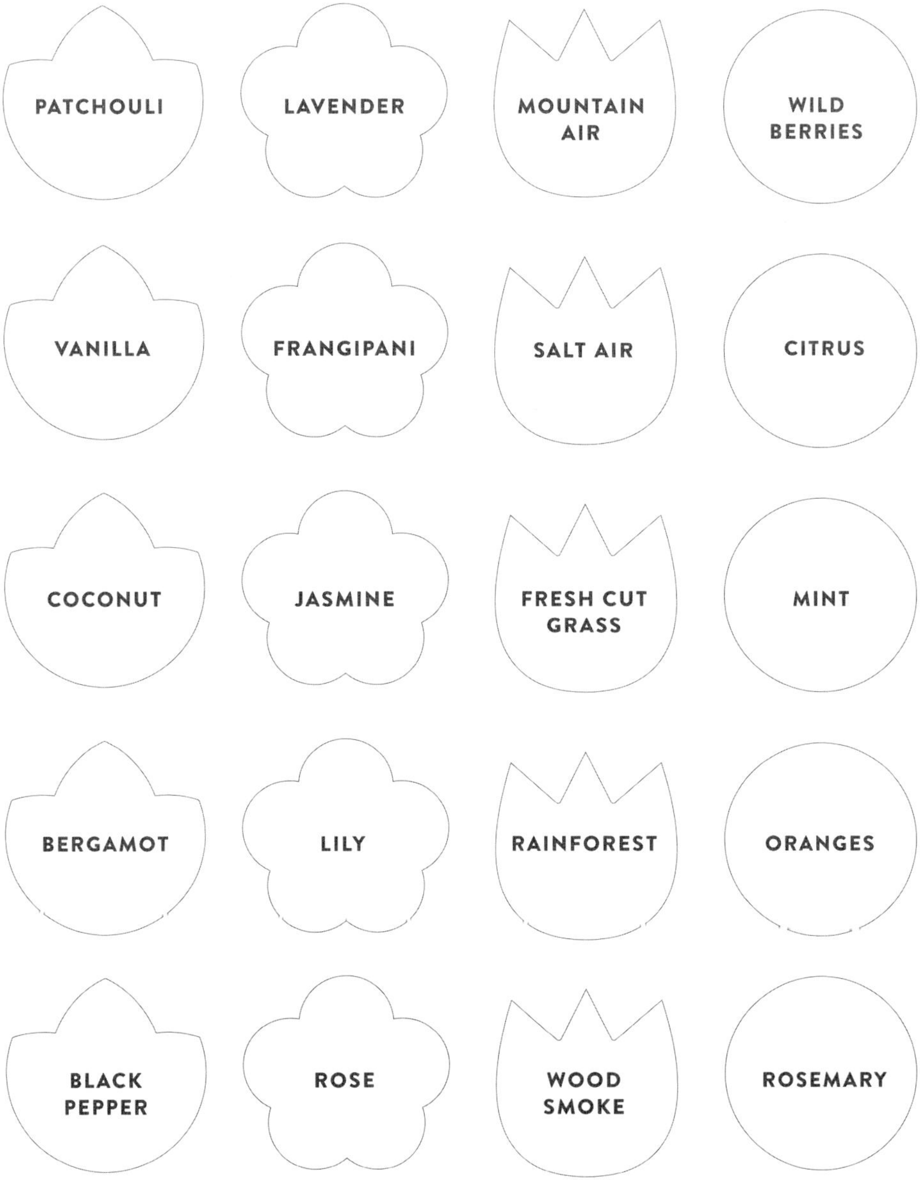
PATCHOULI
LAVENDER
MOUNTAIN AIR
WILD BERRIES
VANILLA
FRANGIPANI
SALT AIR
CITRUS
COCONUT
JASMINE
FRESH CUT GRASS
MINT
BERGAMOT
LILY
RAINFOREST
ORANGES
BLACK PEPPER
ROSE
WOOD SMOKE
ROSEMARY

MY SUMMER FRAGRANCES

MY AUTUMN FRAGRANCES

MY WINTER FRAGRANCES

MY SPRING FRAGRANCES

'Some days
I need the music,
some days
I need the lyrics.'

ANONYMOUS

Music to my ears.

Some people like constant noise, some people like silence. By finding the right tunes you can be lifted up when you're feeling down, calmed when you are manic, or soothed into slumber.

Music and sounds are known to have healing power, so they should be carefully considered in the mix of your self-care routines. Let's explore how music fits in for you.

MINDFULNESS MOMENT

What can you hear?

Feeling stressed, mind going a million miles an hour? A simple mindfulness exercise can help you to tune into one of your senses.

What can you hear?

Stop.

Set a timer for two minutes.

Pull out a pen and paper (or use the page opposite) and write down everything you can hear.

HOW DOES MUSIC FIT INTO YOUR LIFE?

Considering how music fits into your life is important in understanding how it can stimulate, calm and energise you.

Let's answer a few questions.

Do you intentionally put music on?

How often?

Is this enough for you?

If not, what stops you from doing it more frequently?

How can you make it happen?

When do you most like listening to music?

Where do you most like listening to music?

Do you play your own music?

If not, do you wish you did?

How can you make it happen?

Do you see live music?

If not, do you wish you did?

How can you make it happen?

What's your go-to song when you need to be motivated?

What song brings you joy?

What song or sound brings you a sense of calm?

What's the best song to sing along to?

What's the best album to clean the house to?

What's your favourite music to listen to in the car?

What song always makes you sentimental?

All-time favourite album?

Create new playlists.

Creating your own playlists makes sense so that you have access to the tunes you need to fit your mood when you need them. It's a simple organisational tool that can make listening to music easy.

Use the space on the following pages to create a playlist packed full of songs to motivate or calm you. Or use Spotify or your fave music app to create playlists on any topic, vibe, theme or angle you can think of. You can also create playlists in collaboration with others if sharing makes you happy.

If you are stuck for inspiration, why not ride on someone else's coattails and find a ready-made playlist to suit your mood? Simply use the search bar in Spotify to find what you are looking for.

PLAYLIST TO MOTIVATE

PLAYLIST TO CALM

New music challenge.

What an amazing world we live in when you can listen to any kind of music the world has imagined, from electropop to Buddhist monk chants or orchestral symphonies whenever you like at the click of a button (and for free if you don't mind the ads). Do you take advantage of this? Are you curious about new music or do you stick to tried-and-tested all-time favourites? Can you break some ruts in your thoughts, your mood, your ideas by listening to new music?

Try to find the answers by completing this weekly challenge.

1. Each day schedule a time (or be open to seizing a moment when it arises).
2. Think of what mood you would like to create by your music choice.
3. Type that word into the search panel of your music app and see what comes up.
4. Choose a song from the results and if you like it then go on and listen to the full album.
5. Fill in the chart opposite to track your results.

	ARTIST	ALBUM	MOOD	ADD TO PLAYLIST?
DAY 1				
DAY 2				
DAY 3				
DAY 4				
DAY 5				
DAY 6				
DAY 7				

'We all eat,
and it would be
a sad waste
of opportunity
to eat badly.'

ANNA THOMAS

You are what you taste.

Food is a hot-button issue for many if not most of us. Not only is it a territory where negative emotions such as guilt, despair and self-doubt can tend to lurk, it is also, conversely, where we have the capacity to heal ourselves. Food is medicine and it has a sizeable role to play in self-care.

In this section of the journal, you will assess and reassess your attitudes towards food and learn to embrace all the food, glorious food that you love.

How do you feel about what you eat?

Food. And eating. It's a biggie. Everyone is different. And because this journal is about self-care and not diet, the focus is on how you feel about food.

On the page opposite, quickly write down all the foods you eat on a regular basis. Consider the range of food you might eat in a week. You can write the meal itself, eg pad thai, or key ingredients. Whatever works.

Consider your list. Give it a rating from 1 to 10 (10 being a happy little Vegemite) on how good you feel about your current diet. Write it in the circle at the bottom.

If you're on the high side that's great. Keep doing what you are doing.

If you're on the low side, why is that? What can you change?

If you rated yourself a 7 or above in the exercise on the previous page, use this space to write down what you think you are doing well. Refer back here if you feel yourself wavering, or going off track.

If you rated 4-6 use the space to write what you're pleased with but also what you would like to change.

And if you rated below 4, write a kind and reassuring letter to yourself – or simply tell yourself that it's okay that you are not where you'd like to be, and that you are motivated to make changes.

'Follow your feelings.
If it feels right,
move forward.
If it doesn't feel right,
don't do it.'

OPRAH WINFREY

Take control of your food choices.

We all have foods that make us feel guilty if we have them too often. So we can choose to resist temptation, eat and enjoy (perhaps in moderation), or eat and feel guilty. This is a choice. Good self-care means being aware of this choice and taking responsibility for it.

In the top half of the circles opposite write down foods that you love but that make you feel 'bad' when you eat them.

You can either be specific – eg Tim Tams or you can be general – chocolate biscuits.

Now consider each one individually. Think about the bad vibes that you associate with that item. Assign it a rating from 1 to 10 (with 10 being stuff-the-wrapper-under-the-couch bad). Write that number underneath.

Review each food and associated thoughts or feelings and consider if there is space to change the emotions relating to it. Ask yourself 'Can I let go of the guilt associated with eating this and enjoy it for what it is?' If the answer is yes write in in the YES column on the following page. If the answer is no, write that food on the NO column on page 152.

'Only good people feel guilt.'

ANONYMOUS

Say goodbye to guilt and hello to peace.

By acknowledging your acceptance of this food in your life, your feeling towards it can shift, bringing you lightness and freedom, making for a happier life.

On the opposite page is a letter to recite to each of your YES foods. You can use this letter or use the space below to write your own. Go on, talk to your favourite food. Welcome it back – guilt-free – into your life.

MY YES FOODS

Dear ....

I choose to keep you in my life. I no longer battle with you, instead I take you as you are. I respect you and your influence over me, but I remain in control, and I choose to be friends with you. I don't overindulge in you, nor do I argue with myself over your place in my life. You are what you are, and I love you for that.

Yours, ...

Say goodbye for now.

The NO foods are the ones you can't find your peace with. Not at the moment. Maybe one day but not right now.

If eating a Tim Tam – even just one – is going to bring on the guilts then you have to be firm. It has to go. And not because it is damaging your waistline or your blood-sugar levels, but because of the emotional energy that is getting in the way of you caring for yourself.

Thank it, and then let it go.

Say aloud the letter on the opposite page (or write your own in the space provided). Go on, banish the food and banish the guilt. You are back in control.

MY NO FOODS

Dear ....

Thank you for existing, and for giving me moments of joy, but the time has come for me to move on. You are no longer in my life. I wish you no disrespect but the emotion that you bring to my life no longer serves me and I must bid you farewell.

Yours, ...

Foods to love.

What are your favourites? What makes your taste buds sing or makes you feel like running a marathon?

There are certain foods that are known to energise the body or help it to rebuild. Food is medicine, after all.

But what makes you happy?

Write a wish list of foods on the page opposite. For now hang the expense or other practicalities like availability and just brainstorm what you love.

Then next to each food write one of the following four emotions:

Satisfied – Bam. Hunger gone. No need for more.

Motivated – I've eaten something nourishing that I know is nutritious and my body is doing a happy dance inside.

Balanced – I feel relaxed, calm and level. I can concentrate on the task at hand and am able to focus.

Comforted – Ah, yum, that hit the spot and gave me a familiar sensation of feeling soothed and sated.

Against each of your chosen foods write either S, M, B or C.

FOODS I LOVE ...

MAKES ME FEEL ...

FOODS I LOVE ...	MAKES ME FEEL ...

FOODS I LOVE ...	MAKES ME FEEL ...

Create your food top 10s.

Now that you 've got a clear idea of the foods that you love, write a top 10 list for each category using the space provided on the following pages.

Make sure your 'go-to drawer' (at home or at the office), pantry or fridge/freezer is well stocked with your favourite things.

TOP 10 SATISFYING FOODS

TO PUT IN MY GO-TO DRAWER

1. ____________________
2. ____________________
3. ____________________
4. ____________________
5. ____________________
6. ____________________
7. ____________________
8. ____________________
9. ____________________
10. ____________________

TOP 10 MOTIVATING FOODS

TO PUT IN MY GO-TO DRAWER

1. ____________________
2. ____________________
3. ____________________
4. ____________________
5. ____________________
6. ____________________
7. ____________________
8. ____________________
9. ____________________
10. ____________________

TOP 10 CALMING FOODS

TO PUT IN MY GO-TO DRAWER

1. ____________________

2. ____________________

3. ____________________

4. ____________________

5. ____________________

6. ____________________

7. ____________________

8. ____________________

9. ____________________

10. ____________________

TOP 10 COMFORTING FOODS

TO PUT IN MY GO-TO DRAWER

1. ____________________

2. ____________________

3. ____________________

4. ____________________

5. ____________________

6. ____________________

7. ____________________

8. ____________________

9. ____________________

10. ____________________

'Did you say exercise?
Or extra fries?'

ANONYMOUS

'I'm sorry for what I said when I was hungry.'

ANONYMOUS

Don't get hangry!

If you're someone who gets hangry (that's H for hungry and A for angry) don't let this get in the way of your self-care goals. It's okay! Just because XYZ can go all morning without a snack doesn't mean you have to. Listen to what your body is telling you and act on it.

List below five snacks you need to keep within easy reach if you're prone to hanger pangs.

1. ____________________

2. ____________________

3. ____________________

4. ____________________

5. ____________________

Eat well.

Like good sleep, good nutrition is a foundation stone of self-care. Eating well boosts both your physical and mental health.

You probably know the drill: eat the rainbow (all the colours of fruit and vegetables), shop the aisles at the supermarket where the fresh produce lives, watch your portion sizes, don't eat in front of the TV, eat less sugar and more good fats.

Do it – because like drinking water, eating well is a simple but powerful act of self-care.

FOUR GOLDEN RULES FOR NUTRITIONAL SELF-CARE

1.

Limit refined sugar

One simple way to reduce your sugar intake is to not buy packaged food. And another is to occasionally replace processed white sugar with sugars that will be kinder to your body, such as coconut sugar, raw honey, maple syrup or sweeteners like stevia and Natvia.

2.

Decrease refined carbohydrates

Refined or simple carbs are basically sugars and starches that don't exist in nature, and eating them has been linked to heart disease and diabetes. Focus on reducing your consumption of sugar, white bread and pasta.

3.

Focus on your gut

The gut is home to 90 per cent of your body's serotonin – the nifty little neurotransmitter that helps control your mood, sleep and appetite. The gut also acts as a barrier, keeping harmful bacteria out and good bacteria in. When this barrier gets inflamed (called leaky gut) it can wreak all kinds of havoc on your health. For a healthy gut limit or avoid gluten and dairy.

4.

Increase healthy fats

All fats were not created equal. Celebrate the good (unsaturated) fats, which are found in plentiful supply in avocados, fish, nuts, eggs, seeds and some grains. These foods boast high levels of omega-3 fatty acids that are thought to help reduce cholesterol levels and reduce inflammation, among other health benefits.

Grow some herbs.

Growing your own herbs is such an easy way of feeling connected – direct from Mother Nature to your dining table. Fresh herbs enliven the taste buds and add flair and flavour to your cooking.

Tick off your favourite herbs from the list opposite and make a plan to cultivate a patch in your garden or a pot on the balcony. Herbs don't need a lot of space.

Another nifty feature of herbs is that the more you use them the more they grow – so don't save them for later, use them today.

Or just give them a little sniff on your way past – that's pretty nice too.

FAVOURITE HERBS NOT ON THIS LIST

PARSLEY

SAGE

FENNEL

CHIVES

MINT

ROSEMARY

CHAMOMILE

BAY LEAVES

DILL

THYME

TARRAGON

PEPPERMINT

BASIL

CORIANDER

LAVENDER

OREGANO

'Design is coming
to grips with one's real
lifestyle, one's real
place in the world.
Rooms should
not be put together
for show but to nourish
one's well-being.'

ALBERT HADLEY

I spy with my little eye.

A happy home environment that jibes with who you are as a person is a critical element of self-care. We generally spend a lot of time at home, and it has the capacity to bring peace and joy or frustration and dissatisfaction.

What you see around you day in and day out affects how you feel, and you have the ability to make it work for you not against you.

Use the exercises on the following pages to explore how you feel about your home, then adjust as necessary.

If only...

Let's fantasise. Close your eyes and imagine your ideal house. Enter your fantasy home. What do you see first? As you walk through, what objects or spaces make you happy and why?

Perhaps there is a great place to put your shoes or hang your bag (function can be such a simple pleasure). Keep walking: perhaps you spy a lovely artwork on the wall, a generous table for eating family meals, eclectic treasures from your travels on a shelf, books that you can dive into on a whim, photos of friends or family reminding you that you are connected, a piano or a selection of instruments, hanging or glossy-leaved plants, scented candles for relaxing.

Move through the whole house. Consider what objects or items you are filling your fantasy house with. Why are you choosing these things? Are they in your current house? And, if not, can they be?

Use the questions that follow to explore what you can learn about how to create a home environment that is uniquely nurturing for you.

MY HOME – FANTASY VERSUS REALITY

Think about the visualisation you did on the opposite page and answer the questions below.

WHAT WAS ON THE WALLS OF YOUR FANTASY HOUSE?

WHAT ITEMS OR OBJECTS DID YOU SEE AROUND YOU?

WERE THERE LOTS OF PLANTS?

WAS IT MINIMALIST?

WHAT MADE IT COMFORTABLE?

WHAT ITEMS REFLECTED YOUR PASSIONS OR YOUR HOBBIES?

ANYTHING ELSE?

SIX HOME SPACE GOALS

Look at what you've just written and write six goals below that you can pursue over the next month to bring these insights into your current home. Write your goals in detail: don't just say 'more plants', list the kind of plants and where you want them. The more detail you put, the more likely it is that it will happen.

1.

2.

3.

4.

5.

6.

Write your home manifesto.

Consider the words opposite. Do they resonate with you? If so, you could use them as your home manifesto. Or have a go at writing your own, focussing on the things that matter most to you.

Stick your manifesto in a high profile spot as a reminder of what is important, and what home means to you.

MAY THIS HOME BE FILLED WITH THE SOUND OF LAUGHTER AND GIGGLES, FRIENDS NEW AND OLD, *sunshine and light*, ADVENTUROUS STORIES AND TALES, *happy memories to treasure*, FAMILY FROM NEAR AND FAR, FUN AND MAKE BELIEVE, COMFORT AND LOVE, *truth and honesty*, FASCINATING IDEAS AND CONVERSATION, *love and kindness*, HUGS AND KISSES.

See clean, be clean.

Having visitors over or family to stay is often the motivation needed to give the house a good clean. Why is that? Are they more important than you are? Absolutely not. You might not deem it necessary to have the house spotless all the time, but up to the level of 'good friends over' should be the bare minimum. And perhaps not just the warts-and-all good friends, because you want to raise the bar a bit, right?

On the self-care scale, the act of cleaning scores high on discipline and low on joy for most of us. But the output – a clean and tidy environment around us – is way up there, so your focus should be on getting it done as easily and efficiently as possible. So make a plan.

HOW TO PLAN TO CLEAN

A master cleaning schedule provides structure, enabling you to do a daily whip around to stay on top of things, while also designating specific days and times to get bigger jobs done. Download a cleaning schedule from the internet or make your own.

1.

Decide what to clean daily.

Make a checklist.
Put it on the fridge.
Schedule a time for it.
Do it.

2.

Decide what to clean weekly.

Make a checklist.
Put it with your household admin paperwork.
Schedule a date and time for it. Write it on the calendar.
Do it.

3.

Decide what to clean monthly.

Make a checklist.
Put it with your household admin paperwork.
Schedule a date and time for it. Write it on the calendar.
Do it.

What's with the clutter?

If you don't have clutter, yay you. Pat yourself on the back and move on to the next page.

For most of us though, clutter is a fact of life. You know it. It's there. And it's not going anywhere unless YOU take charge.

Let's get to the heart of the problem. For some it's a lack of time (or is that an excuse?), for others it's sentimentality, and for others it's just not enough space or a lack of organisation. Understanding the core issue can help you find the best solution.

Think about a space in your house that feels crowded and unmanageable. It might be an entire room, a cupboard even just a drawer. Now use the space opposite to have a little rant. How annoying is this space? Is it someone else's fault? Why can't you get on top of it? Get it all out. And breathe.

Deal with clutter.

Phew. Does that feel better? Read what you wrote in your rant and try to be objective. Are you making excuses? Is there something new you can try?

Look at the tips opposite, and consider which ones can you can employ to help make your place streamlined and clutter free.

TIPS FOR EASY DECLUTTERING

1. Put on some good music, light an aromatherapy diffuser, wear comfy clothes, open the windows – and get sorting!
2. Know why you are doing it – approach the job with a positive mindset focussed on the joy decluttering will bring to you.
3. Start small – with one specific and manageable area, such as your junk drawer.
4. Set a timer – never more than 30 minutes for the first few times.
5. Use three boxes and label them 'In,' 'Out' and 'I Don't Know'. Ensure there is a place for the in items, discard the out items and place the don't knows in a sealed box in the shed. Review in six months.
6. Discard with gratitude. Thank the item and give it away if you can (rather than putting it into landfill).
7. Never start your decluttering with sentimental objects.
8. Observe the 'one in, one out' rule.
9. Buy less stuff.
10. Set up a workable and practical system to repeat this exercise regularly and stay on top of your decluttering.

Get organised in 12 random steps.

1.

Always leave your keys and phone in the same place. Always.

2.

Make your bed in the morning and do the dishes before you go to bed at night.

3.

Make a new to-do list every single day – base it on the previous day's list and anything that came up since then.

4.

Delegate tasks to other members of the household if possible.

5.

Make a master grocery list, which contains a complete list of all the foods and household necessities you use. Refer to it each time you prepare your shopping list, cross referencing with your weekly meal plan and what you have in the pantry, fridge or freezer.

6.

Practice *mise en place* (putting in place). This culinary term is inspired by chefs who are experts at keeping small spaces clean and organised. Learn from them.

7.

Put things away in their place immediately. Do not dump them on a chair, kitchen bench, etc. Encourage others to do the same.

8.

Prepare a budget and find a way to track it that works for you.

9.

If it's broken, fix it. Having broken stuff around is dispiriting and makes you feel bad, so unless there's a real reason not to, get it fixed, or get rid of it.

10.

Unsubscribe from mailing lists, newsletters, magazines and anything else you don't use or need. Mental clutter – be gone.

11.

Prepare a weekly meal plan and stick to it.

12.

If you feel overwhelmed, just do one of these things. And give yourself a pat on the back.

Tackle your finances.

Financial self-care. It's a thing. And it's not the $100 a month you set aside for your gym membership. No, it's creating a firm financial foundation for your life. Just as you look out for your emotional and physical health, financial well-being is key to your self-care plan. If you're stuck where to start, try just talking about money – with your partner, friends or financial specialists. Get the conversation started and you'll bring energy and focus to the topic. Set financial goals, tackle debt with an action plan and build a budget. Reframe the agenda so that instead of money having control over you, you have control over it.

Use the space opposite to identify five things you are going to do over the next two weeks to manage your finances. Chose significant things that once achieved will make you want to give yourself a big high five. You can do it.

1.

2.

3.

4.

5.

'Enjoy your body.
Use it every way you can.
Don't be afraid of it or of
what other people think of it.
It's the greatest instrument
you'll ever own.'

ANONYMOUS

Let's get physical.

So far in this journal we've covered four of the five senses: taste, hearing, smell, sight. The fifth sense is touch.

Let's think of this as being in touch with your physical body – your one true home. Loving, honouring, nurturing and respecting your body is a fundamental component of self-care.

Exercise!

The very word strikes fear into the hearts of some and sounds like a bucket load of fun to others. Regardless which camp you fall into, the evidence is beyond doubt. Exercise is really good for you, it may help combat disease and even prolong your life. Those are maybes, but what's certain is that it will make you feel better.

For many people it's a matter of finding what works for them – the type of exercise, the time of day, the company and the location. All of these things make a big difference to whether or not you enjoy the exercise you do and ultimately whether or not you stick with it.

Look at the questions on the opposite page. Jot down your answers alongside. Use the answers to help you home in on the types of exercise that work best for you.

1. Do you prefer to exercise alone, with one other person or in a group?

2. Are you a morning, lunchtime or evening exerciser?

3. Do you like aerobic exercise, or prefer strength or endurance training?

4. What are your exercise goals – general fitness, building strength, weight loss, flexibility, social interaction, etc?

5. Do you prefer to exercise indoors or outdoors?

6. Do you prefer to have a set schedule or to mix it up?

7. Are you self-motivated or do you need a trainer or app to gee you along?

8. Was there a physical activity you loved as a kid? Fancy giving it another try?

9. Do you need to be mindful of budget? If so, choose something that's free or very cheap (it's possible).

10. Are you currently fit or not really? Choose something you can achieve without an epic struggle.

Stuck for ideas?

If you're bored of your current exercise regime and need to mix it up a bit, or you need a bit of inspo to get started, take your pick from this list of ideas that make exercise fun. Colour in the ones that sound good.

BUY A KAYAK

GO FOR A SWIM
Make it a daily ritual if you can

BUY SOME RESISTANCE BANDS AND DO HOME STRENGTH TRAINING

PLAY WITH THE KIDS
Run, jump, dance, cut loose

SIGN UP FOR AN OBSTACLE COURSE RACE

PLAY FRISBEE IN THE PARK

LEARN TO SURF

SKATEBOARD

JOIN A RUNNING CLUB

JOIN THE CIRCUS
Or go to the beach and practise your cartwheels

GO TO BOOTCAMP

JUMP ON A TRAMPOLINE

DO THE HOUSEHOLD CLEANING WITH EXTRA GUSTO

HAVE A WALKING MEETING
Instead of the usual boardroom type

GO FOR A WALK IN THE FOREST
Pick a hard trail with lots of hills

GO TO A DANCE CLASS

TRY CAPOEIRA

TAKE AN ONLINE YOGA CLASS

JOIN A ROLLER DERBY TEAM

JOIN THE TEAM
Whether it's a work team or in your community, consider soccer or netball

GO STAND UP PADDLE-BOARDING

GET OUT A SKIPPING ROPE AND JUMP

SQUAT WHILE YOU WATCH TV OR BRUSH YOUR TEETH

GO FOR BIKE RIDE
See how fast you can go

TRY ROCK CLIMBING

LEARN POLE DANCING

TAKE UP A MARTIAL ART
Judo, karate, tai chi or quigong

BUY A HULA HOOP
And work that thing

DO A 30-SECOND (OR MORE) PLANK DAILY

Practise breathwork.

Bring your attention to the breath. It's good advice. When we place our attention there, we tend to breathe more slowly and deeply, letting the breath go on a journey through and around the body before exiting. Our heart rate and blood pressure slow, our muscles relax, we feel calm. The shift from shallow to deep breathing facilitates this and is a great skill to learn to help you relax.

Breathwork can also be a mindful and deeply spiritual practice. It has been known to help those with mental health problems, and to shift any mental 'stuckness' or unhelpful thought patterns. At its most transcendental, breathwork can help you connect to the universe as you learn to let the life force, or prana, of the universe flow through you.

MINDFULNESS MOMENT

SLOW BREATHING EXERCISE

Stand or sit quietly. Take a normal breath and hold it. Count to six then breathe out and in your mind say the word 'relax' as you exhale. Breathe in for three seconds, then breathe out for three seconds, repeating the word 'relax' on each exhale. At this pace, you will take 10 breaths per minute. At the end of the minute, take another normal breath and hold for six seconds. Then repeat the exercise.

Practise this slow breathing technique for five minutes at a time, four times a day.

Relax those muscles.

We naturally tense our muscles to perform everyday tasks in a competent and alert manner. The problem is that we then fail to 'switch off' these muscles, and they become wired to tension. Over time we get used to it and fail to notice the presence of tension or, more importantly, the absence of its counterpart, relaxation.

This tension can cause physical problems, such as headaches or back pain, as well as feelings of jumpiness and anxiety. So it is very important to learn to relax our bodies. By relaxing our bodies, we regain control over our minds and can better deal with anxiety.

MINDFULNESS MOMENT

FULL BODY RELAXATION EXERCISE

Sit in a comfortable chair, or lie down flat on your back.

Close your eyes and then slowly tense and relax each major muscle group.

Hold the tension as tightly as you can (don't worry if you get a little shaky) for 10 seconds per muscle group.

Release for six seconds, noting the feeling of tension leaving the body.

Concentrate on the difference in how your muscles feel before and after – this is key to the exercise.

This progressive muscle-relaxation technique has been shown to help people with anxiety.

""Go to bed, you'll
feel better tomorrow"
is the human version of
"Did you try turning
it off and on again?""

ANONYMOUS

Sleep.

Ah, sleep. What a problem it can be. Getting enough sleep is, for a lot of people, a tricky thing. All sorts of things get in the way, be it a baby that wakes up at 4.30am, work concerns, noisy neighbours, money worries, endless chores before bedtime – and so on.

Remember to consider sleep within the parameters of your life – and be kind to yourself. If you have responsibilities such as small children that keep you up at night, don't beat yourself up over not getting enough sleep. That doesn't help. The point is do you get as much sleep as you can? Are you maximising the time available? If you are looking at social media late into the night and then blaming the baby, you may need to fess up!

Sleep is important. And the good news is that there are lots of things you can do to help ensure you get the best night's sleep possible.

Create a rest-inducing night-time routine.

Setting a night-time routine is an important step in setting yourself up for a restful night's sleep. Whatever works for you is the best routine for you. It might come down to a bit of trial and error so experiment with these or other ideas that appeal before deciding on your night-time routine.

1.

Go to bed early (and around the same time each night).

2.

Leave electronic devices out of the bedroom or set to 'do not disturb' if you must have them there.

3.

Create an optimum environment: quiet, dark and cool. (Buy block-out curtains or an eye mask.)

4.

Do a sleep meditation before bed, or write down your worries in a notebook.

5.

Wear intentional nightwear, not an old pair of shorts and a singlet.

6.

Don't go to bed too full, or hungry. Avoid alcohol and caffeine.

EVERY NIGHT I WILL:

Waking up.

Waking up from sleep can be problematic for some people, while others bound out of bed ready to set the world on fire. If you are someone who struggles to leave the sleepy slumber or to find motivation for the day, then having a morning routine can certainly help. Knowing exactly what you need to do and doing it on autopilot can offset low mood or lethargy.

For those in the other camp, the 'morning people', make sure you capitalise on your good fortune. Set this time aside for something constructive, don't let it slip away and then regret it later when you're all tuckered out at the other end of the day (or even by lunchtime!).

CREATE YOUR MORNING ROUTINE

Think about how you would like your morning to flow. Would it be the same every day, or is variety important to you? What is the first thing you do in the morning? What is the first thought you'd like to have in the morning? How can you turn around unwanted thoughts that might crowd your head on waking?

Use the circles opposite to create your own unique morning flow chart. Write into the circles five ideas and the order to do them.

Here are a few ideas you could consider or brainstorm your own until it feels right.

Meditate for five minutes.

Do a short yoga sequence.

Say my affirmation.

Write down my goal for today.

Write down three things and one person I am grateful for.

My morning flow chart

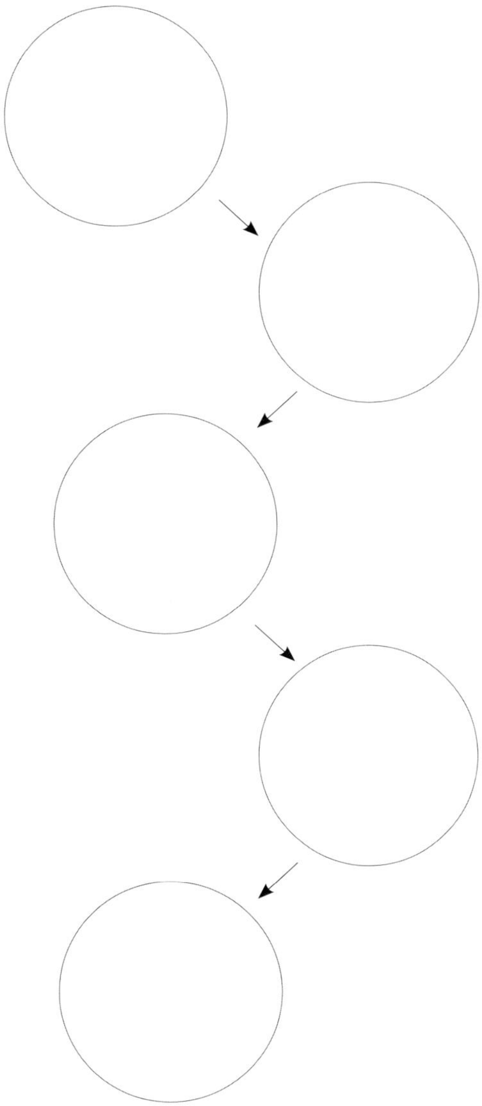

'You should sit in
meditation for 20 minutes
a day, unless you are
too busy, then you
should sit for an hour.'

ZEN PROVERB

The sixth sense.

The ultimate aim of any spiritual journey is surrender and acceptance – to what is and what will be. It's a peaceful state to be in, which will enable you to flow sweetly and easily with life. It takes effort, like all good things.

There are lots of way to explore and channel your spiritual side. Explore, research, practise – and enjoy the journey.

1. Gain awareness through mindful meditation.

2. Know yourself and your intentions.

3. Be graceful and kind to all beings.

Nurture your spiritual side.

Who or what can help you along the way? Consider the options and commit to learning more about what interests you. Where your energy goes, results will flow.

I WANT TO LEARN MORE ABOUT

CRYSTALS	MEDITATION
TAROT	BREATHWORK
SPIRIT ANIMALS	CREATING A SACRED SPACE
ENERGY HEALING	DEEP LISTENING
AROMATHERAPY	MANDALAS
ACUPUNCTURE	SACRED TEXTS
CHAKRAS	VISUALISATION
MINDFULNESS	KINESIOLOGY

'You can't buy
happiness but you can
buy crystals
and that's kind of the
same thing.'

ANONYMOUS

Spirit animals.

A spirit guide is a messenger or teacher that has a personal connection with and relationship to you. Certain cultures believe that we travel through life with a group of spirit guides illuminating our path. Animals are one of these.

There are many possibilities, but some of the more popular animal spirit guides are featured on the opposite page.

Every animal has attributes that we can identify and learn from. For example, the fox can teach us how to tackle problems and get around obstacles in a new way. The lion teaches us assertiveness and self-confidence and challenges us to deal with unnecessary stores of anger. The elegant swan will guide us to discover and appreciate our own beauty and to employ good grace in dealings with others. The horse reminds of our power, energy and individuality. It teaches that 'I can'.

Follow the tips on the next pages to tune into and identify your spirit animal, and then you can learn more about it and how to listen to its messages.

SWAN

Realise your own
true beauty

FOX

Walk safely down
your destined path

LION

Take control of
the situation

WHALE

Listen to your
inner voice

HORSE

Express yourself freely
and openly

PEACOCK

Be confident in
your actions

EAGLE

Feel empowered
to make decisions

BUTTERFLY

Transform with
lightness and grace

WOLF

Find order out of chaos

MINDFULNESS MOMENT

What is your spirit animal?

How do you know your spirit animal? There is no way to know with certainty, but there are ways to tune in and discover.

Close your eyes and imagine you are an animal. What comes to mind?

During meditation, bring your awareness to this issue. What animals emerge? Accept what comes up.

Observe your dreams. Do any animals appear strongly or repeatedly?

Observe your surroundings and the words of others. Do certain animals keep appearing in the flesh or in conversation?

Ask your spirit animal to reveal itself to you. You could do this in the context of a simple ceremony to call in your spirit animal.

Be in nature. When you are next walking in nature, take extra care to hold close the smells, sounds and feeling of the life around you.

If you are interested in an animal, research and learn about it.

Simply tune in: what animal resonates most deeply with you? Let it guide you. Open your heart to its messages.

WHAT CAN YOU LEARN FROM YOUR SPIRIT ANIMAL?

You spirit animal is a guide. It's purpose is to help you bring attention to parts of your life that may need further understanding and focus and to point you in the right direction, with new skills to move forward.

Take time to research and reflect on the qualities, habits and interactions of your spirit animal. Be clear about what resonates with you. And then seek to assimilate these elements into your own life. As you do this, you will naturally deepen the sacred bond that you hold with this animal, and open yourself up to its deep wisdom.

When you meditate, bring your animal spirit guide to mind regularly and ask it for guidance. Learn to listen to the messages and direction it is giving you.

3

SELF-CARE CARDS

This section of the journal contains 52 little ideas and exercises for self-care. Overseas travel, career success and glamorous parties are great, but life is lived in the day to day, the little things and small moments. And it is here where we have the most potential to make decisions that enable us to care better for ourselves.

'Great things are done by a series of small things brought together.'

VINCENT VAN GOGH

52 little (but big) ways to look after yourself.

On the 'cards' that follow, you'll notice that there is a heart, circle and cross at the bottom of each idea. Colour in the icon that fits best for you. If it's a definite for your self-care plan then colour in the heart, if it's a maybe, colour in the circle and if it's a no, colour the cross.

Now you have a handy quick reference guide for improving your self-care.

Stretch

Like food, water and the air we breathe, stretching is good. It keeps your muscles flexible, strong and healthy. It helps your blood flow and calms the mind. You can do it before you even get out of bed in the morning. Or set yourself a simple five-minute stretching routine to do while the sun rises. It's a wonderful way to start your day. If you work at an office, stop and stretch. If you don't work at an office, stop and stretch. You get the picture.

Put your legs up in the air

It's known in yoga as Viparita Karani (or Legs Up the Wall Pose). And it's got to be the pose that delivers the biggest bang for your stretchy buck. It's easy. It doesn't hurt. It only takes 15 minutes at most (and less is fine). And it's soooo good for you. It calms the nervous system, quietens the mind, relieves tired legs and feet, and eases back pain. Find a time to do it daily and reap the rewards. Set a reminder on your phone if it helps.

A little bit of knowledge goes a long way

Learn more about how your body works, whether that's the speed of your metabolism, your gut health or hormonal balance. If you understand your body better, it becomes easier to know what it needs and how best to care for it. You can learn through observation, research or seeking professional help, such as from an integrated health practitioner, healer or nutritionist.

Soak up some rays

Sunshine is nature's bubble bath: it's relaxing and it makes you feel good. And it's actually doing you good. Getting out in the sunshine for just 10 minutes a day three times a week will boost your vitamin D levels enough to improve bone health and your immune system. Sun exposure also increases levels of serotonin. Known as the happiness hormone, it does what it says on the tin. The more sunshine in the daytime, the more melatonin you produce at night, helping you have a better night's sleep. If that's not enough, recent studies have made a link between sunshine and weight loss. It seems a few extra rays can reduce body fat and help you shed the kilos.

Share food and gratitude

At the dinner table tonight take turns in sharing an experience – something that happened today for which each person is grateful. Make this a dinner-time ritual.

Pack lunchboxes with love

When packing your kids' lunchboxes for the third time this morning, the 21st time this week and the gazillionth time this lifetime, consider being grateful for this moment, for the opportunity to care and tend to your loved ones and to nourish them with healthy food.

Write a meal plan

Deciding what to have for dinner is a drag. Chucking out limp veggies from the fridge is wasteful. Why put yourself through it? It's easy to design a weekly meal plan. You may even want to do it monthly: when you're in the zone, you might as well. Rotating recipes regularly makes the task easier. Designate a day each week to do your planning and your grocery shopping. Cook twice as much as you need and have the leftovers for lunch. That way you only need to plan for one meal a day, plus breakfast and snacks.

Drink your coffee

Choose your favourite mug. Notice where in the world the coffee grains have come from. Observe the smell and the noise as your coffee brews. Fill the mug and pick it up, noting its warmth. Take a sip. Savour its smell and rich, earthy flavour. Notice the sensation in your mouth. Slowly but surely begin to tune into your day. That's right: drink your coffee mindfully.

Turn your bathroom into a spa

Sometimes you just need to run a bubble bath, light a scented candle and shut the bathroom door on the world. Go the extra mile and put on face mask or other body treatment if you feel like it. Make sure you have spa-worthy, clean, fluffy towels, and nice slippers and a robe to put on afterwards. And, relax. #costsnothing

Dress up

How you look shouldn't matter and it doesn't really, but let's face it, sometimes it makes you feel simply invincible to do your hair and make-up, put on your favourite or most glamorous clothes and look the world right the eye. If you feel that way, do it. You don't need a reason.

Buy yourself something nice

It's okay to treat yourself now and then. Try tapping into your needs and desires. Sometimes we want to buy something for the quick hit of pleasure that it brings, which is often followed by remorse. But if it's something you've had your eye on for a while and your budget can cope with it, then why not?

Do your nails

For some people, doing their nails is a Zen-like experience. It requires concentration and the result is pleasing (hopefully). Through the repetitive motion of nail painting, we hush hush our minds and any potential negative self-talk. Nail painting is a simple gesture that says 'I am worth it'. Unless you are doing something fancy like nail art, it is a small, easily accomplished task that has immediate results.

Care for your plants

Houseplants are so on trend right now. They look amazing and they are good for your health. They do the opposite of what we do when we breathe – they release oxygen and absorb carbon dioxide, freshening the air and eliminating nasty toxins. Taking the time to select and look after your houseplants is a simple, beautiful act of self-care.

Pick some lavender

If you are lucky enough to have lavender growing in your garden (and if you don't, plant some – it's easy to grow), then harvesting it and putting it to good use is therapeutic. After the lavender has dried (this takes about a week) you can use it to cook with (think lavender syrup or buttercream), to make bath salts, to make lavender bath bombs or wands (google it – a great project to do with the kids), as a drawer-deodoriser or simply as a decoration in the home. Lavender is so versatile and its earthy, pungent smell is invigorating.

Take a forest bath

Government-backed research in Japan has shown the health benefits of taking a stroll in the forest. (A formal therapy developed from the research is known as *shinrin-yoku*, which translates as 'forest bathing'.) It's incredibly simple – really, it just involves walking very slowly in the bush and observing all the sounds, smells and sights of nature. If you feel distracted, simply stop, sit still and listen more closely. You might even notice how the trees are communicating. This activity has been proven to lower the heart rate and calm the body's flight or fight response.

Walk barefoot

Otherwise known as 'earthing', walking outside barefoot has been medically proven to improve sleep, reduce inflammation and increase antioxidants. Studies have shown that our feet respond the electrical charges in the earth, and when we are in direct contract with these, we benefit. So kick off your red suede shoes and go soul-to-sole with Mother Nature.

Make time for each other

As we race through life in a flurry of kids, work, sports and essential appointments, it's easy to forget about the one we love the most. Sometimes we might even forget why we love them the most. But it's a flame that's usually easy to reignite. Make plans: a surprise date, a regular date, any kind of date. If getting out of the house is too hard, even a date at home would work (think candlelit dinner). A good relationship with a partner is second only to a good relationship with yourself. Don't neglect it.

Send a love note

Write a love note and mail it to your other half. Or put it in his wallet or lunchbox. #awww

Give to others

A growing body of research shows that giving to others has a positive impact on your physical and mental health. It could be a gift, a donation to charity or a random act of kindness such as paying for someone's coffee or meal.

Call an old friend

Call someone you've lost touch with for no real reason, or someone you haven't spoken to in a while. Sometimes it's hard to do, but it always feels great.

Get involved

It takes just a couple of minutes to pick up the phone or send an email and say 'Yes' to getting involved in an event in your community. It might be helping out at the school or an organisation you already belong to. Or maybe it's something completely new that caught your eye in the local paper. Getting involved in the community where we live improves our sense of belonging, helps us to build meaningful relationships with neighbours and can provide purpose and meaning to our lives.

Make plans with someone

It's nice to have social events to look forward to in the calendar. If your calendar is a bit too empty for your liking, then make some plans. You could invite your co-workers out for lunch or a drink, plan an adventure with a good friend or a romantic date with your other half.

Stay connected

Stick to your regular appointments. If you have meetings with your parents' group, community group or other social group don't let your attendance lapse because you are too busy. If you don't have meetings like this, try setting up a regular coffee date with a friend, or schedule an evening a week to call a friend or family member.

Put some books in a footpath library

You've seen those cute little boxes filled with books that appear at random on nature strips? Somebody took the time to make and/or erect your local footpath library. So give it some love: pop in a book or two next time you've finished one or are having a clear out. If you take books from the library, there's an unspoken rule. Take one, give one back.

Start a mood tracker

Emotional self-regulation is important to self-care, but it can be hard to pinpoint our feelings if we don't pay careful attention. Plus, most of us ride the roller coaster of emotions rather than stop, pause and think about what's going on. Using a mood tracker can help. It's helpful to see our emotions represented visually and empowering to see changes, and how far we've come over time. Whether it's custom made, store bought, or an app, a mood tracker is a tool that can help you take care of yourself and make improvements to your daily life.

Practise gratitude

Gratitude is strongly associated with increased levels of happiness. Start practising it today by writing a gratitude list. It doesn't need to be exhaustive – start with five or 10 things.

Sometimes it might feel that gratitude flows from the pen, but other days it will be hard to summon anything much to be thankful for. If that happens, be grateful to yourself for even trying.

Start a feel-good file

Whether you choose to make a document on your desktop or just an old-school folder, the idea is to create a place where you can collect happy memories, photos, complements you have received, great experiences, hopes, wishes and dreams. Have a look through it when you need a boost or a bit of inspiration.

Use journaling prompts

Keeping a daily journal of your thoughts, what worries you and what inspires you, is one of the best productivity tools there is. But if you find yourself staring at a blank page, try journaling prompts. These are targeted questions can help you start writing when you're stuck for inspiration. Often it's only a little push we need to get going.

Don't focus on being nice

It's not your job to smile at strangers, join in conversations, like posts on social media or agree to participate in things you don't want to do. Remember that.

Take a moment for your mantra

Set your intention for the day by repeating your chosen mantra. Bond with your mantra and make it your own. You can chant it, speak it out loud in front of the mirror or write it down.

Create a bucket list

Bucket lists are cool because they make us stop and think what we actually want to experience in our time on planet Earth. They remind us that this time is short and to make the most of it we need to be proactive. Here's how to do it. Set aside 15 minutes and grab a piece of paper. Now, brainstorm without limits. Write down everything that comes to mind. That's your bucket list. Go back to your list either in the same session or another time and refine it. Set a timeframe (by decade if you like) and prioritise your top three, five and 10 bucket list items. Share the list with a buddy if you like and even designate activities you'd like to do together.

Stay warm

Go the extra mile in winter to make your bedtime the pleasure it should be. Put your pyjamas in the tumble drier for five minutes before putting them on. Put a hot-water bottle in your bed 10 minutes before you turn in. Snuggle in bed with a warm cup of herbal tea, your journal and/or a good book. #sweetdreams

Eat a banana split

If you want a banana spilt, eat a banana split. Life is to be enjoyed. Small pleasures are important. Provided you don't only eat banana splits, it will be okay.

Don't forget to play

Play is where we are free to be ourselves, make mistakes, dream big, act silly, laugh and connect with others. Everyone secretly just wants to play, so find your thing, create your own games or activities and watch others get on your bandwagon. Or to make it really simple, next time you are catching up for coffee with a friend, suggest that you do some craft activity together, or go kick a ball in the park. If you're on your own in the park and you want to go on the kids' swing, do it.

Do a burst of body movement

Do something fun (or silly) to get your heart racing. Run up and down the stairs, chase the kids round the garden, do a crazy dance. Just a few minutes at a time done regularly can radically improve your health. See if you can make your short bursts add up to 20 minutes a day and you'll be kicking some serious healthcare (equals self-care) goals.

Laugh

Laughter has physiological effects – lowering blood pressure, boosting T cells, strengthening the heart and flooding the body with feel-good endorphins. So don't resist a great big belly laugh if you feel it coming on.

If laughter comes easily to you, lucky you. If it doesn't, consider laughter therapy (or laughter yoga), which are structured ways of helping trigger the funnies. Don't let the weirdness of it get in the way of the benefits.

Whistle...

Or hum or sing or laugh. When we do these things our body comes into balance. The jaw unclenches, the facial muscles relax, the lower back and legs feel lighter. Just try, a little hum, a little whistle or song. Force it out and keep going. Joy will have its way with you eventually.

Do art and don't care

To practise the art of not giving a s**t, which is a fundamental skill to have in your self-care toolkit, experiment with doing something creative such as a painting or a piece of writing and not caring whether it's good or not. You can chuck it right in the bin if you like. Who cares? Keep on practising until you feel your inner judge-on-high-of-all-that-is-perfect just slip-slidin' away.

Dance

When it all gets too much, put on some loud music and dance like nobody is watching. You can do this anywhere but the kitchen is a good place. Spin like a whirling dervish (watch the stove!), dress up in tea towels and croon into a wooden spoon.

Do something crafty

Beading is meditative. It enables you to focus and be fully absorbed in the task of creating something beautiful. It can also improve fine motor skills and lower blood pressure, making it a nifty activity for restless kids too. Same goes for crochet, weaving, drawing, colouring in – etc. So make time for a bit of craft in your life. Hold a 'crafternoon' – it's a great thing to do with friends on a rainy day.

Schedule your distraction

Love a funny cat or cute baby video, or is a hit of hard news more your style? Whatever it is that you enjoy, rather than defaulting to it whenever you feel your mind wandering from its task, set a recurring daily event in your calendar. Ten minutes should do the trick. Then go cat-video-crazy.

Go out and take photos

Taking pictures on a digital device is a part of everyday life. It's become a reflex action, done without much thought. Try thinking about it. Take a small number of photos (limit yourself to a number, say three or five). Choose your subject carefully and really look at it before you take the photograph. Taking a photograph attunes us to our environment, improves memory and helps us to focus on positive or meaningful experiences. You chose to photograph something beautiful, right?

Meditate for five minutes

You can meditate whenever you like, or get a chance, but research suggests that first thing in the morning is the ideal time. Its benefits are maximised when the mind is clear, free from the stresses of the day. You can meditate for however long you like, but five minutes is fine and a great start. Build up from there if you want to. Why bother? It will help to set you up for the day, generating an overall sense of calm and well-being, and enable you to tackle the day with greater focus and energy.

Take screen breaks

Be mindful of your dependency on your phone or social media. If you're struggling to stop scrolling, ask yourself why? What's going on with you?

Put some simple strategies in place to manage it. Turn off your email and work phone outside of work hours. Take an hour screen break, by scheduling 'do not disturb' in the settings on the phone. This will put a stop to messages, calls and notifications for the time you allocate. Try not to have multiple screens open or access to more than one screen. Do one thing at a time, even if it is looking at your phone.

Throw out the random socks

You could keep a basket of single socks on top of your washing machine waiting for their partners to show up some time. Or, here's a better idea: let them go. If the idea really pains you, then look online for sock reuse ideas – golf-club protectors, hand puppets, bird feeders, that kind of thing.

Are you really going to read that again?

Books can be hard to let go of, but they take up a lot of space and gather dust. If you're not going to re-read it, refer to it as reference, or pass it on to a friend, then set it free. Give it to your local charity shop or footpath library. Let someone else love it as much as you did.

Do a digital cleanse

Take 15 minutes to do a digital cleanse. Tackle an overcrowded desktop. File what needs to be filed and delete the rest. Be one of those people with a picture of a mountain or a sunset on their screen – and that's it. Take the same ruthless approach to your phone and other devices. Delete and/or unsubscribe from apps you don't use. Get rid of text messages you've been hanging onto (why?) and back up your photos and videos. (While you're at it, make a folder of 10 of your absolute favourite photos.) You'll free up storage, potentially save money and feel heaps better.

What even is that?

You know that drawer where you put things that you don't know where else to put... Go to that drawer. Take everything out and organise it. Try to find suitable homes for items that seem lost. If you can't find a home for it, then ask yourself, 'Do I really need it?'. If the answer is no, then get rid of it. Recycle or give it to the op shop if you can, and if not, apologise to the earth, declare your ongoing desire to be a more responsible consumer, and let it go to landfill.

Edit your to-do list

Have a look at your to-do list. Is it really necessary to do everything on there? Be ruthless and get rid of any non-essential tasks from the list. Next, subdivide the bigger tasks and the smaller ones, and put them in priority order. Then put a plan in place for how and when you are going to deal with them.

Take care of small tasks

Small tasks are cumulative in nature. They build up, causing a drain on the brain and unnecessary stress. Don't ignore them. Instead find ways to tackle them effectively. If it takes less than two minutes to complete a task, take care of it right away. Slightly more complicated tasks, or multiple tasks, will need to be addressed differently. Designate a block of time in your weekly calendar when you can do them. Try to batch tasks that can be done together, for example at a single location (your computer perhaps) or on a walk to town.

Recap the day

Before you turn off the light at night, write down your favourite three things from the day.

Make a time capsule

Gather together a few items, such as photos, inspirational quotes or small objects (that you can part with) which reflect your current life. Write a note describing where you are at right now. Include facts such as where you live and with whom, and also reflect on how you feel about your life – any particular challenges or triumphs or day-to-day niggles. Put it all into a nice box or jar, close the lid and tuck it away somewhere safe.

4

IT'S A WRAP

In this journal, the end truly is the beginning. Here is your chance to pinpoint and summarise what you have learned in completing this journal, and to set priorities for how you plan to take better care of yourself in the future. And the future starts now.

'Celebrate your success
and stand strong when
adversity hits, for when the
storm clouds come in,
the eagles soar while
the small birds take cover.'

NAPOLEON HILL

Now what?

If you've got this far, you've done a lot of work. Well done you.

Some people like to obsessively monitor and track their progress. (You can find some great tools online for this.) Others like to be a bit more fluid in their approach, but either way it's good to keep track, otherwise you can miss big and little milestones along the way, and you don't want that.

In this section of the journal you'll find some simple tools to help you remember the commitments you made in this journal and the ideas that you explored.

Self-care is a life's work, because you never stop learning about yourself and your needs can change over time. So keep thinking about your self-care and in your busy life, find a way to prioritise yourself. Because you matter.

Who are you?

Hopefully you should now have a clear idea about what changes you need to make to welcome more self-care into your life.

What has been working so far and what needs to change?

Using the circles opposite, take a snapshot of where you are at right now. (If you think you'll find this a useful exercise, you might want to photocopy these pages first and then you can repeat it whenever you want to.)

Write the top three activities you currently do that support your attributes (see pages 32-33 for a refresher).

Write the top three wish list activities that support your desired emotional state (see pages 56-57 for a refresher).

Write three things you can do to nurture your values (see pages 66-75 for a refresher).

TOP THREE ACTIVITIES THAT SUPPORT MY ATTRIBUTES

TOP THREE WISH LIST ACTIVITIES

THREE THINGS I CAN DO TO NURTURE MY VALUES

MY 'HEART' ACTIVITIES

Here is a reminder list of all the ideas and exercises from Section 3 of the journal that you gave a heart to. Refer to this list when you need a reminder of these activities, and use the boxes provided to note tick off when you have done them.

'You serve the best by doing what you love the most.'

MARIA BELLO

Simple weekly tracker.

The questions on the following page have been created to reflect the ideas that you've worked through in this journal.

Use them as a simple tracking tool. Tracking is important as a way of keeping goals, commitments and priorities that you have made for yourself in the forefront in your mind.

You can either colour in the circle if your answer is a yes, or put in a rating from 1 to 10 to indicate how successful you feel you have been in that area this week, with 1 being not very and 10 being absolutely smashed it.

Doing one activity per week towards a big goal is enough, but if you stay focussed smaller changes can more easily become a new daily habit. Using the tracker will help you stay aware of whether or not that's happening for you.

If three weeks go by and no boxes have been filled in then it's time to consider how more time and space can be made for your self-care.

	M	T	W	T	F	S	S
Am I making my sleep situation as positive as possible?	○	○	○	○	○	○	○
Have I embraced my morning routine?	○	○	○	○	○	○	○
Did I do an activity that supports my attributes?	○	○	○	○	○	○	○
Have I done one of my wish list activities?	○	○	○	○	○	○	○
Have I done an activity that nurture one of my values?	○	○	○	○	○	○	○
Have I progressed one of my S.M.A.R.T. goals?	○	○	○	○	○	○	○
Have I stopped negative self-talk by reinforcing positive affirmations?	○	○	○	○	○	○	○
Did I do something to nurture my soul?	○	○	○	○	○	○	○
Have I respected my right to say no?	○	○	○	○	○	○	○
Have I surrounded myself with smells that make me feel good?	○	○	○	○	○	○	○
Have I listened to new or favourite music?	○	○	○	○	○	○	○
Have I made supportive food choices?	○	○	○	○	○	○	○
Am I happy with my surroundings visually?	○	○	○	○	○	○	○
Did I nurture my physical body?	○	○	○	○	○	○	○
Have I expressed myself creatively without passing judgement?	○	○	○	○	○	○	○
Did I do something to honour my cleaning schedule?	○	○	○	○	○	○	○
Have I watered my plants?	○	○	○	○	○	○	○
Have I done something towards better planning or budgeting?	○	○	○	○	○	○	○
Have I done something to declutter or be more organised?	○	○	○	○	○	○	○
Have I practised my evening routine?	○	○	○	○	○	○	○

'Talk to yourself like you would to someone you love.'

BRENÉ BROWN

NOTES

NOTES

HERRON

First Published in 2021 by Herron Book Distributors Pty Ltd
This Edition Published in 2022
14 Manton St
Morningside
QLD 4170
www.herronbooks.com

Captain Honey
WWW.CAPTAINHONEY.COM.AU

Custom book production by Captain Honey Pty Ltd
12 Station Street
Bangalow
NSW 2479
www.captainhoney.com.au

Cataloguing-in-Publication. A catalogue record for this book is available from the National Library of Australia

ISBN: 978-1-922432-94-0

Printed and bound in China

5 4 3 2 22 23 24 25